A Christian Understanding of the
Jewish Holidays:

A HANDBOOK

HJR Cohen

No part of this book may be reproduced, stored in a retrieval system, or transmitted by any means, electronic, mechanical, photocopying, recording, or otherwise without written permission from the author.

Copyright © **HJR Cohen** 2023. All rights reserved.

All rights reserved. This book or parts thereof may not be reproduced in any form, stored in any retrieval system, or transmitted in any form by any means—electronic, mechanical, photocopy, recording, or otherwise—without prior written permission of the publisher, except as provided by United States of America copyright law.

ISBN:
Softcover: 9781988557922
Hardcover: 9781988557939
Ebook: 9781988557946

First printing edition in 2023
Published in the United States of America
by Three Ravens Media

This book is written for all believers who enjoy exploring the Word of God, embracing new insights, and experiencing more of our Creator. The sentiment behind this book is one of joyous privilege—that God so chose to make these holiday appointments with us.

I want to personally dedicate this book to my family:

My oldest son: a strong young hero; my comfort
My youngest son: a precious gift who warms my heart; my joy
My daughter: a bubbly spring of life and giving; my delight
My mother: my fun, supportive, inspiring mum; my best girlfriend ever

And foremost,
My spouse, my best friend, my treasure and rock.
Your passion for knowledge, encouragement, generosity and tenderness are unsurpassed.

Todah raba to Rabbi Dr. John Fischer. This book may not have happened at all without your guidance and expertise. May your fountain of knowledge continue to bless countless others for generations to come.

Contents

Introduction 1
Biblical Holidays (*Moedim*) 8
Jewish Calendar 12
New Moon (*Rosh Chodesh*) 16
Sabbath (*Shabbat*) 21
Passover (*Pesach*) 51
Feast of Unleavened Bread (*Matzot*) 72
Feast of Firstfruits (*Bikkurim*) 82
Israeli Memorial Day (*Yom HaZikaron*) 86
Israel's Independence Day (*Yom Ha'Atzmaut*) 88
Feast of Weeks and Pentecost (*Shavuot*) 92
Feast of Trumpets (New Year's Day or *Rosh Hashanah*) 102
Days of Awe (*Yamim Noraim*) 118
Day of Atonement (*Yom Kippur*) 120
Feast of Tabernacles or Booths (*Sukkot*) 136
Eighth Day of Assembly (*Shemini Atseret*) 156

Rejoicing of the Five Books of Moses (*Simchat Torah*) 156

Feast of Dedication or Festival of Lights (*Chanukah*). 164

Birthday of Trees (*Tu B'Shevat*). 177

Feast of Lots (*Purim*). 181

Holocaust Remembrance Day (*Yom HaShoah*) 192

Fast of the Ninth of Av (*Tisha B'Av*) 195

Conclusion. 199

Weekly *Parsha* Reading Schedule. 200

Bibliography and Suggested Readings 203

INTRODUCTION

Christianity is a child of Judaism. If you are a Christian, your faith has Jewish roots. Christians follow Jewish texts (yes, not just the Older Testament, but even the Newer Testament is technically Jewish literature). Christians follow Jewish ethical models—the most famous being the Ten Commandments given through Moses. Christians follow the writings of a Jewish rabbi commonly known as Paul, and more importantly, Christians follow a Jewish Messiah.

An accurate understanding of Christianity, therefore, relies upon one's understanding of the Jewish culture and the Semitic theology of the Church's foundations. This includes, to a very great extent, the holidays and feasts of the Bible. Often ignored in Christian circles, these holidays are unwrapped gifts free for the taking. They compliment and enhance the Christian interpretation and understanding of the world's Redeemer. These holidays map out the divine plan of salvation, redemption and God's relationship with His people. A Christian cannot afford to miss out on the beautiful and timeless lessons designed for our benefit by the very hand of God.

These Jewish holidays are in themselves a treasure trove of meaning, rich with lessons and full of symbolism that can provide invaluable insight and exciting new paths in the spiritual walk of a Christian. In this book, I would like to explore the holidays of the Bible and the Jewish people. I include a description of each one featured here as well as discuss some of the traditional methods of observance and how the holiday can benefit the Christian reader. I would like for this resource to be used as a guidebook for the Christian in his/her exploration of these feasts, fasts and memorial days.

Following, is a chart containing a very brief synopsis of the major and minor holidays featured in this book. Notice that even each minor or "secular" Jewish holiday holds its own significance. For this reason, I have included them in this assortment.

AVOIDING CULTURAL APPROPRIATION

In today's world, concerns of "cultural appropriation" are valid. Christians can engage with Jewish holidays and biblical ritual objects in a respectful and culturally sensitive manner. To enjoy this book and its contents as a Christian, remember that you can do so without fear of cultural appropriation by remember these things:

- **Educate Yourself:** Take the time to learn about the significance, history, and meaning behind the Jewish holidays and ritual objects you're interested in. Understand the cultural and religious contexts in which they hold importance. (This is the intent of this book).

- **Show Genuine Interest:** Approach Jewish traditions with an authentic desire to understand and appreciate rather than to exploit or trivialize. Engage in conversations with Jewish friends, read relevant literature, and attend educational events to deepen your knowledge.

- **Participate with Respect:** If invited, participate in Jewish holidays or ceremonies with respect and humility. However, do so as a guest and observer, following the lead of those who are more familiar with the customs.

- **Do not prosletyze:** Often Christians feel the need to prosletyze or 'witness' without having been asked about beliefs in the first place when being a guest in a Jewish setting. This is disrespectful, rude, and most likely will not have the intended outcome you may wish for. If, however, a Jewish person comes to your church, then it is appropriate to tell them about your beliefs and that of the church's.

- **Avoid Stereotypes:** Refrain from perpetuating stereotypes or making assumptions about Jewish culture based on superficial knowledge. Avoid caricatures, jokes, or behaviors that may be disrespectful or offensive. Even simply referring to Jews as "smart" or "succesful" or "rich" or "running things" may seem harmless or even complimentary, but they are faulty stereotypes and have been the cause of much antisemitism, resentment, and hatred, and thus such statements are therefore considered antisemtic as well.

- **Acknowledge Origins:** When discussing or enjoying Jewish holidays or objects, acknowledge their origin and significance. It's important to give credit where it's due and recognize that these customs are from a specific culture and religion.

- **Cultivate Relationships:** Build relationships with members of the Jewish community, seeking their guidance and perspectives. Engaging in conversations can provide valuable insights and help you understand the nuances of the traditions.

- **Respect Boundaries:** Understand that some aspects of Jewish culture and traditions are deeply personal and may not be appropriate for outsiders to engage in. Respect any boundaries or limitations set by the community. While boundaries between Christianty and Judiam are to be respected, this book intends to help the Christian understand Judaism better in the context of appreciating both the roots or Christianity and understanding better the culture of their Jewish Messiah. The Christian may be grafted into the chuch of the Messiah of Israel, but the Chrstians as a whole never 'replace' or 'supplant' the Jewish people, and this must be emphasized. While some important scriptures are shared, each have their own role in God's kingdom.

- **Avoid Commercialization:** Be cautious of turning Jewish holidays or ritual objects into commercial ventures or fashion statements. This can trivialize their significance and be perceived as insensitive.

- **Share Knowledge:** If you're a Christian who wants to share your experiences with Jewish holidays or objects, do so in a way that promotes understanding and respect. Sharing what you've learned can contribute to cross-cultural appreciation.

- **Reflect on Intentions:** Before engaging with Jewish customs, consider your motivations and intentions. Are you genuinely seeking to understand and appreciate, or are you looking to appropriate for ultterioer motives such as to better prosletyze or to 'gain' in some way other than seeking deeper religious undersatnding for your personal spirituality? This is very important.

Remember that cultural appreciation involves humility, empathy, and a genuine desire to learn. It's about celebrating and understanding cultural diversity rather than exploiting it. By approaching Jewish holidays and ritual objects with a spiritual respect and mindfulness, Christians can enjoy and engage with these aspects without causing offense or cultural appropriation. So, with no further adieu, enjoy!

HOLIDAY	WHAT IS IT ABOUT?	CHRISTIAN SIGNIFICANCE	WHEN?
Sabbath (*Shabbat*)	Commemorates God's rest after Creation as well as His covenant with Israel	Fellowship with God & rest in New Earth	weekly
New Moon (*Rosh Chodesh*)	New month & time for introspection	Gives reference point for calculating holidays as well as a "miniature *Yom Kippur*" [time for introspection and repentance]	monthly
Passover (*Pesach*)	Israel's miraculous exodus from Egypt & escape from death, first-born salvation by the blood of the Passover Lamb	Escape from sin; salvation from eternal death through the blood of the Heavenly Passover Lamb	Mar/Apr
Feast of Unleavened Bread (*Matzot*)	Israel's hasty departure from Egypt (no time for bread to rise)	The unleavened (sinless) body of the Messiah broken for our sins, predecessor of the bread of the Eucharist	Mar/Apr
Feast of Firstfruits (*Bikkurim*)	Beginning of the spring barley harvest & offering this "first" harvest to Temple	Resurrection of Yeshua after death—the "first" of the harvest of the resurrection	Mar/Apr
Counting the Barley Sheaves (*Omer*)	A forty-nine day count beginning from Firstfruits & leading to the Feast of Weeks	Time beginning from resurrection of Messiah & leading to Feast of Weeks/ Pentecost	From Passover to the Feast of Weeks
Israeli Memorial Day (*Yom HaZikaron*)*	National holiday to remember fallen soldiers	If not for the sacrifice of the fallen, there would not be a State of Israel today	Apr/May
Israel's Independence Day (*Yom Ha'Atzmaut*)*	Commemorates the day that the modern State of Israel became an independent nation	This is the real birthday of modern Israel—a prophetic fulfillment to many	Apr/May
Day thirty-three of Omer Count (*Lag B'Omer*)*	Respite from somewhat solemn Omer period	Day of fun to enhance solidarity with Jewish nation—picnics, archery, haircuts	Apr/May
Feast of Weeks and Pentecost (*Shavuot*)	The giving of the law at Mt. Sinai to include the Ten Commandments written by God's own finger upon tablets of stone	Pentecost—the anniversary of the receiving of the Holy Spirit as described in Acts 2	May/Jun
Feast of Trumpets (New Year's Day or Rosh Hashanah)	Anniversary of Creation*** & repentance for sealing of souls in the Book of Life for the year	New Creation & Second Coming of Messiah & sealing of souls in the Book of Life for eternity	Sep/Oct

HOLIDAY	WHAT IS IT ABOUT?	CHRISTIAN SIGNIFICANCE	WHEN?
Days of Awe (*Yamim Noraim*)*	Time for introspection for annual renewal	Time for introspection for eternal renewal	Sep/Oct
Day of Atonement (*Yom Kippur*)	Atonement of sins made through ceremony of animal sacrifice	Atonement of sins made through sacrifice of the Messiah	Sep/Oct
Feast of Tabernacles or Feast of Booths (*Sukkot*)	Dwelling of God with humankind in the wilderness	Dwelling of God with humankind in the form of the Messiah	Sep/Oct
Eighth Day of Assembly (*Shemini Atseret*)*	Focus on the spiritual relationship with God—corporate and individual	Focus on the complete relationship with God in eternity—corporate and individual	Sep/Oct
Rejoicing of the Five Books of Moses (*Simchat Torah*)*	Rejoicing of the word of God & our relationship with the word	Rejoicing of the Word of God & our relationship with the Word	Sep/Oct
Feast of Dedication or Festival of Lights (*Chanukah*)*	Rededication of the Temple & miracle of Maccabee victory and lasting oil	Rededication of ourselves as Temples of the Spirit of God	Nov/Dec
Birthday of Trees (*Tu B'Shevat*)*	Time for planting trees	Time to plant good deeds in our lives	Jan
Feast of Lots (*Purim*)	Israel's victory over Haman (and genocide)	Victory by an invisible God	Feb/Mar
Holocaust Remembrance Day (*Yom HaShoah*)*	Remembering the millions of Jewish Europeans killed during World War II (Let their memory never be forgotten)	Awareness of anti-Semitism and its dire consequences	Apr/May
Fast of the Ninth of Av (*Tisha B'Av*)*	Reflection and grief over hardships faced	Hope during hardship due to God's mercy	Jul/Aug

*= Minor, modern Israeli and/ or non-biblically mandated holidays
*** The attributing of the "Anniversary of Creation" to Rosh Hashanah is a rabbinical tradition and does not necessarily appear in scripture, but due to symbolic significance and plausibility, is mentioned in this book.

It is my intention that this book will inspire joy and fulfillment in the hearts of the readers who are hungering for a greater knowledge of their Messiah and of the festivals and holidays that surround his mission for humanity.

BIBLICAL HOLIDAYS (MOEDIM)

WHY KEEP THEM NOW?

In the latest decade, study-guides and books line shelves of Christian book centers focused on Biblical and/or Jewish holidays. Why? Why would a Christian be interested in these holidays if they are 1., for those of the Jewish faith only, or 2., outdated and "done-away with?" The Christian culture has divorced itself from Judaism almost two thousand years ago, so the holidays and feasts that were observed and cherished by the disciples and Jesus [Yeshua][1] himself have become foreign and distant to most of the Christian world until recently. A stirring among Christianity is awakening many to the beauties and rich symbols of the biblical and/or Jewish holidays.

God Himself[2] ordained and/or sanctioned many of the festivals, feasts and fasts present on today's Jewish calendar. Since these days are not merely the invention of humanity, perhaps it would do Christianity well to become acquainted with them. The remaining holidays on the

---

[1] I will refer to Jesus by his Hebrew-Aramaic name, "Yeshua," (sometimes interpreted as "Yehoshua") unless quoting directly from another source. "Jesus" is an Anglicized name that he would never have actually used or even *heard* in his own lifetime. "Yeshua" means literally "Salvation." The name "Jesus" is an interpretation of this twice removed (first to Greek and then to English). It's not wrong to use "Jesus," but I prefer "Yeshua."
[2] For the sake of simplicity, I will be referring to God in the masculine form. I am by no means implying that God is a "male" as in the human understanding, since both male and female are created in the image of God.

Israeli calendar are also rich in meaning and also beneficial for learning and Christian growth.

God set these *moedim* (holy days) aside to meet with his people. Like a bridegroom setting a special day aside to meet with His bride, God is ready to meet with His people on these sanctified days. It is the *choice* of His people therefore, whether they choose to meet with Him or to pass on the opportunity altogether.

Rabbi Shaul, the pharisee better known by the Christian community as Apostle Paul, adds more insight into the holidays as we read his writing regarding the feast of Passover:

> *Your boasting is not good. Don't you know that a little yeast works through the whole batch of dough? Get rid of the old yeast that you may be a new batch without yeast—as you really are. For Christ, our Passover lamb, has been sacrificed. <u>Therefore let us keep the Festival</u>, not with the old yeast, the yeast of malice and wickedness, but with bread without yeast, the bread of sincerity and truth.*[3,4]

Here Paul himself is encouraging his audience to keep the feast, but with more sincerity than before. *He is by no means outright discouraging the observance of Passover or any other feast.* He is advocating its perpetuation with spiritual enrichment and sincerity. He keeps on with the observance of the day himself, as this account describes: "But we sailed from Philippi after the Feast of Unleavened Bread, and five days later joined the others at Troas, where we stayed seven days."[5] Notice he uses the Feast of Unleavened Bread (part of the Passover week) as a time reference. This would have been totally redundant if neither he nor his audience observed the day—especially since he is in the diaspora. He uses

---

[3] I Corinthians 5:6-8 (emphasis added)
[4] Since my intended audience for this book is Christian, all scriptures are taken from the New International Version unless stated otherwise.
[5] Acts 20:6

"the Fast" as reference also. We can only surmise it is *Yom Kippur*, the most important fast of the year: "Much time had been lost, and sailing had already become dangerous because by now it was after the Fast..."[6] We can safely say that, contrary to popular Christian belief, the Jewish holidays were quite in effect in the Early Church and were observed by the first Christians of the time. Perhaps John Fischer said it best and succinctly:

> The B'rit Hadasha (Newer Testament) stresses that Yeshua (Jesus) fulfills the message of these calendar events, providing them with added significance. Hebrews (8:5; 10:1) speaks in terms of them being "shadows of good things to come," that is, they highlight the Messiah. But a shadow can't highlight anyone if it's removed from the picture. Therefore, the "shadows" still have important functions to perform. Yeshua taught (Matt. 5:17-19) that anyone who annulled the least of God's commandments, or taught others to do so, would be called "least" in His kingdom. He didn't come to abolish or set aside the Law and its teachings; he came to do the opposite, to fulfill them. The term Yeshua used for "fulfill" carries the idea of bringing to full expression... (Fischer, 2004, accessed 04 Aug 2010).

By the excerpt above, we can see that scripture is clear in stating that these Sabbaths or festivals are "shadows" of things to come. They point to important events in the future of God's people. For example, Passover points to Yeshua, the Passover lamb. The Feast of Trumpets points to the Second Coming of the Messiah—a future event. When God addressed the nation of Israel, He had to give them a method of remembering the important events that would occur years, centuries and even millennia from that era of Sinai, when all Jewish people were gathered together to

---

[6] Acts 27:9

receive God's instructions. He therefore instituted these feasts and holidays so that His people would observe them weekly, monthly or annually, preserving the message behind them. Each generation was to keep them faithfully for all time so that these, God's people, would keep the timeless message behind the holy days afresh in their minds. These days provide not only an opportunity to remember the actual future events as foreshadowed by the holidays themselves, but also are times that provide opportunity for God to meet with his people now as He did then.

Please note that in no way does holiday observance affect one's salvation. Salvation comes by the grace of God alone. In no way am I advocating that by the observance of these Jewish holidays we can in any way "earn" our own salvation or "gain Brownie points," so to speak. Likewise, if we do not observe these holidays, God is not necessarily standing by to strike us. Legalism is not advocated in true Judaism, true Christianity, or in this book. *The blessings and joys are in the observance of the holidays themselves.* Like the tabernacle of old, the biblical feast days hold many spiritual lessons and symbols pointing to the endless mercy and love of our Creator. These days are here for our examination and are tools whereby we can enjoy an increased intimacy with our God and Savior. For this purpose this book is written.

JEWISH CALENDAR

The Jewish calendar is quite different than our commonly used Christian calendar (originally a solar Roman calendar developed in 45 B.C.E. by Julius Caesar and later modified as a Gregorian calendar by Pope Gregory XIII in 1582). While the Christians' solar calendar has been counting for just over two millennia, the Jewish lunar calendar has been counting for three times that long (almost six thousand years)! Where the former is based upon the earth's 365-day orbit around the sun, the Jewish calendar is based upon the cycle of the moon. As such a calendar, it marks the month's beginning when the moon is new and continues for twenty-nine to thirty days until the moon is waning once again. This lunar calendar was mandated by God to begin with the Passover month.[7] This month is now known as *Nissan*. According to the biblical mandate, "the first day of *Nissan* is the beginning of the year for kings and festivals" while "the first day of *Tishrei* is the new year for the reckoning of years, for Sabbatical years, and for Jubilees" (Mishnah 299).[8]

---

[7] Exodus 12:1-2
[8] Due to harvest cycles, *Tishrei* was the international beginning of the year before God changed the first month to *Nissan/ Aviv* in commemoration of Israel's flight from Egypt.

Name of Month	Number	Length	Gregorian Equivalent
Nissan/ Aviv	1	30 days	March-April
Iyar	2	29 days	April-May
Sivan	3	30 days	May-June
Tammuz	4	29 days	June-July
Av	5	30 days	July-August
Elul	6	29 days	August-September
Tishrei	7	30 days	September-October
Cheshvan	8	29 or 30 days	October-November
Kislev	9	29 or 30 days	November-December
Tevet	10	29 days	December-January
Shevat	11	30 days	January-February
Adar	12	29-30 days (30 in leap year)	February-March
Adar II	13	29 days	March-April

MONTHS

Originally, the months were named for their order such as "First Month" or "Second Month." Later, the months were formally named. Interestingly, many of these components of the Jewish calendar bear foreign names. These were adopted from the pre-Babylonian Akkadian-Sumerian language and civilization. The following chart provides more information on each month such as the origin or meaning of its name and the holiday(s) associated with it. Compare this chart with the one previous to get a full picture of the Jewish calendar months.

Here below lists the Jewish months, their individual origins and interpretation of their names and their respective associated holidays (Steinburg,19):

Jewish Month	Meaning of Name	Associated Holidays
Nissan / Aviv (Spelled also as *Abib*)	From *Nissanu*: meaning "first produce"	Passover Yom HaShoah
Iyar (or *Ziv* in the Bible)	From *Ayaru*: meaning "light and brightness of blossoming flowers" (related to Hebrew word *or*)	Yom HaZikaron Yom Ha'Atzmaut Lag B'Omer
Sivan	From *Simanu*: meaning "to mark" or "appoint" (related to Hebrew word *sim*)	Shavuot
Tammuz	From *Du'uzu*: taken from *Dumuzi*, the Sumerian god of fertility	No holidays
Av	From *Abu*: meaning is uncertain, possibly "father" if related to Hebrew word *abba*)	Tisha B'Av
Elul	From *Ululu*: meaning "to become pure"	No holidays
Tishrei (or *Ethanim* in the Bible)	From *Tashritu*: meaning "beginning"	Rosh Hashanah Yom Kippur Sukkot Shemini Atzeret Simchat Torah

Jewish Month	Meaning of Name	Associated Holidays
Heshvan (also *Marheshvan* or *Bul* in the Bible)	From *Warhu Shamnu* (or *Arakh Samna)*: meaning "eighth month"	No holidays
Kislev	From *Kislimu*: meaning is uncertain	*Chanukah*
Tevet	From *Tebetu*: meaning "to dip" or "to sink;" possibly referring to the mud of the rainy season	No holidays
Shevat	From *Shabatu*; meaning "beating" or "striking:"	*Tu B'Shevat*
Adar	From *Adaru*: meaning is uncertain, possibly "to worry"	*Purim*

LEAP YEAR

The Jewish calendar arranges its months according to the moon, but it does so by arranging all twelve months into the confines of the solar calendar. We know that there were twelve months used in ancient Israel; Solomon had twelve officers in charge of royal supplies, one for each month of the year.[9] Neatly arranging the twelve months into one exact solar year also requires a leap year, as the solar and lunar calendars do not line up exactly. The leap year addition, the month of Adar II, is used for seven out of every nineteen years. This insures that the holidays repetitively occur roughly the same time of year (for example, Passover is always in the spring season), thus rendering the possibility of the Gregorian equivalent(s) as illustrated in the first chart.

[9] I Kings 4:7

NEW MOON (ROSH CHODESH)

On Jewish calendar: first day of each month

Now the LORD said to Moses and Aaron in the land of Egypt, "This month shall be the beginning of months for you; it is to be the first month of the year to you."[10]

HOLIDAY BACKGROUND

The new moon marks the beginning of each new month. The first day of the Hebrew month is a dark, seemingly moonless night. By this sign in the sky, time was initially recorded and marked in Israel. Holidays were calculated according to this *Rosh Chodesh,* or literally, "head of the month." This provided a reference point so that the ancient people could count forward from the new moon, or first of the month, to calculate holidays.

After leaving Egypt, the first commandment given to Israel was to observe and sanctify the new moon, thereby creating the lunar calendar mentioned previously. The first month was to be marked and noted. This was because the determination of the exact time of the holidays was dependent upon an accurate orientation of the lunar calendar which was to be a direct result of an inerrant calculation of the new moon.

---

[10] Exodus 12:1-2 NASB

TRADITIONAL OBSERVANCE

Until sixteen hundred years ago, the calendars used by the common people were unwritten. On the night of the new moon, great bonfires were lit on nearby hilltops so as to be seen by all. This marked the beginning of the month, *Rosh Chodesh*. The calendars were kept "mentally," as the nation counted days forward from this celestial sign each month.

By the Second Temple period, *Rosh Chodesh* was quite a festival. The *Sanhedrin* was appointed as the collective custodian of the calendar, recording faithfully each new moon. Sighting the new moon became quite an occasion:

> Sumptuous meals were prepared in a large courtyard to encourage the people to serve as witnesses to the sighting. They gathered and waited their turn to be interviewed by the religious leaders. Upon examination of two reliable witnesses, the *Sanhedrin* declared, "The new month is sanctified—it is sanctified!" The celebration then began. The people were jubilant as the prescribed sacrifices were offered. Meanwhile, the priest blessed the people [with the Aaronic blessing of Num 6:24-26] (Scott, 1997:11).

With such gaiety of the new moon, a celebration was guaranteed at the beginning of each month. This aided the people in keeping their minds attuned to God's calendar and holidays. The new moon during this time in history rarely passed by without much ado; therefore, the memory of prescribed holy times was brought to the fore each month when the concept of time observance itself was stressed.

We have a scriptural example of traditional *Rosh Chodesh* observance in the time of King Saul. In the textual story, David speaks to Jonathan and mentions his invitation to dine with King Saul for *Rosh Chodesh*, or the new moon.[11] Although David declines the invitation to join Saul's

---

[11] I Samuel 20:5

royal table for this traditional monthly feast, he nonetheless acknowledges the holiday and its observance. One of the psalmists also speaks of *Rosh Chodesh*, with the injunction to "blow the trumpet [*shofar* or ram's horn] at the new moon".[12]

Contrasting with dining gaily or, feasting with jubilation is the second purpose of *Rosh Chodesh* as recognized by some Jews; *Rosh Chodesh* is a miniature *Yom Kippur*, a time of introspection and repentance. With the Day of Atonement coming only once a year, a more frequent periodic opportunity for collective repentance is warranted. Choosing *Rosh Chodesh* as such a time keeps the faithful from straying too far—surely a monthly spiritual "check up" is better than an annual one.

WOMEN AND ROSH CHODESH

Some traditions of Judaism postulate that only men were involved in the sin of worshipping the golden calf of Exodus 32. Women were believed to have refused to participate.[13] In reward for their abstinence from this idolatrous sin, women were given *Rosh Chodesh* as their "day off;" in some Jewish circles, women are not required to work at all on the day. This is the reward for women, the gender who is believed to have boycotted the licentiousness of that infamous incident at the foot of Sinai. Thus, this a good time to set aside some charity support for women's causes.

WHAT DOES THIS MEAN FOR YOU, A CHRISTIAN?

Just like the moon, we live in light and darkness. Whether we are in brightness or heavy blackness, we are God's children and just as much

---

[12] Psalm 81:3

[13] The argument holds that Aaron, in Exodus 32:2, requests the gold earrings from the men, and they are told to get them from their "wives." Since the word "husbands" is not mentioned, it is sometimes assumed that the addressed group was masculine only. Such an argument leaves the wives (possibly "women" altogether) out of the planning of the golden calf and possibly, the sin of idolatry altogether.

part of His plan. We are just as significant as our God's love is for us, regardless of the light we feel or see around us—or even of the light we do not. With our focus on this distinction between light and darkness, we can also benefit from opening ourselves up to more light to lift away spiritual darkness. Shadows of evil, even if perceived as slight and "marginal," may be creeping into our lives. Taking advantage of this opportunity for pause, reflection, introspection and repentance, helps us all keep ourselves in check. This is in hopes that a year filled with monthly self-corrections may prevent us from getting too far off-track as we could if only subjecting ourselves to spiritual examination annually.

HOLIDAY NOSHES (SNACKS)

These cookies have been a smashing hit at our house. They are also great for tea parties and any celebration calling for a delicate aromatic treat. They are classy and cleanse the palette with their floral essences. The subtle lavender and rose put them over the top!

FRAGRANT CRESCENT MOON SHORTBREAD (pareve)

Ingredients

- 2 cups all purpose flour
- 1/2 cup margarine
- 1/3 cup sugar
- 2 teaspoon vanilla or rose water
- 3 tablespoons of water (more or less to attain desired rolling constancy)
- 1 tablespoon dried lavender flowers

Variation

- Omit vanilla, replacing lavender flowers with dried, crushed rose petals.

Directions

1. Preheat oven to 250 F.
2. Mix dry ingredients well, cut in shortening, add moist ingredients and work together into dough.
3. Roll out dough 1/4 inch thick (sandwich dough between layers of plastic wrap)
4. Using an upside down drinking glass, cut out a circle. Using the same glass, cut out part of the circle, making a crescent moon shape.
5. Bake on cookie sheet for 8-12 minutes or just before turning golden brown on top.
6. ENJOY!

SABBATH (SHABBAT)

On Jewish calendar: Sundown of 6th day or Friday night (*Yom Shishi*) to sundown of the 7th day or Saturday (*Shabbat*)

"If you keep your feet from breaking the Sabbath and from doing as you please on my holy day, if you call the Sabbath a delight and the LORD's holy day honorable, and if you honor it by not going your own way and not doing as you please or speaking idle words, then you will find your joy in the LORD, and I will cause you to ride on the heights of the land and to feast on the inheritance of your father Jacob." The mouth of the LORD has spoken.[14]

HOLIDAY BACKGROUND

In the very beginning of the Bible, in the Creation story of Genesis, the Sabbath day is created and sanctified as a day of rest. Scripture describes how God created the universe and its inhabitants in six days. The Creator rested on the seventh day and sanctified it; God set it aside forever as a holy day of rest.[15] The Sabbath day is specified as the last day of the week. It begins like each of the days previous—in the evening with night and day following, basically sundown to sundown. The days are

---

[14] Isaiah 58:13-17
[15] Genesis 2:2-3

described with a definite order of dusk preceding dawn; "the evening and the morning" were what constituted a full day.[16] Sabbath, like the other holidays discussed here, all begin on the evening on what seems to be the day prior. Thus, this weekly Sabbath is an observance beginning every Friday evening and extending until Saturday evening.

God indeed sanctified the Sabbath at Creation, however, the divine ordinance to revere the day was instituted (or perhaps re-instituted) at Mt. Sinai as one of the Ten Commandments written by the divine finger of God:

> *Remember the Sabbath day by keeping it holy. Six days you shall labor and do all your work, but the seventh day is a Sabbath to the LORD your God. On it you shall not do any work, neither you, nor your son or daughter, nor your manservant or maidservant, nor your animals, nor the alien within your gates. For in six days the LORD made the heavens and the earth, the sea, and all that is in them, but he rested on the seventh day. Therefore the LORD blessed the Sabbath day and made it holy.*[17]

This commandment is the only one that begins with the command, "remember." Ironically, of all the Ten Commandments, it is the most "forgotten" today by Christianity. It was made as an everlasting covenant between God and His people. Divine mandate states that the Sabbath is to be kept as a holy day set apart. Anyone who did work on this day was to be put to death.[18] The observance of the day was to serve as a sign, a trademark of God's own invention put upon His people. This was to provide a unique opportunity of fellowship between the Divine and His mortal creation.

---

[16] Genesis 1
[17] Exodus 20:8-11
[18] Exodus 31:14

The Jewish people hail this weekly Sabbath as one of the most important holidays of the Jewish calendar. The seventh-day Sabbath is not to be confused with the other "Sabbaths" of the year. There are seven of these high holy days of the year (two for the Passover [*Pesach*] week, one for Weeks [*Shavuot*], two for Trumpets [*Rosh Hashanah*], two for Tabernacles including the Eighth Day [*Sukkot* and *Shemini Atseret*] and one for Atonement [*Yom Kippur*]). Each one is referred to as a "Sabbath" in a general inference of its holiness and requirement for restful observance. On these Sabbaths, although the people are not to do any work, these days are still not in the same category as the seventh-day Sabbath which stands above all in the context of restfulness. Despite occurring weekly, the Sabbath is to be celebrated with all the awe and excitement of an annual holiday; its frequent celebration should never bring complacency.

Although the mandate for Sabbath is rest, the actual rest is only half of it. The Sabbath is not a vacuum. The absence of work is to create a time of leisure, a time of relaxation and recharging of the spirit. Imagine dropping a heavy load that you have carried all week, finally to be free of it for a whole day. When it comes to Sabbath observance, we must remember that every "no" creates an opportunity for a "yes" (Drucker, 158). Without the obligations of the week, one is finally able to enjoy visiting friends, playing games or reading without guilt of wasting time or being "unproductive." This day is a "home" of peace. It is our happy place we can escape to each and every week.

TRADITIONAL OBSERVANCE

Traditionally, Jewish people begin to observe Sabbath quite a bit earlier than its "actual" sundown arrival on Friday night. Friday, the "preparation day," is an extended part of Sabbath observance; this day is designated to provide the opportunity to ready the home and family for the onset of the holy Sabbath. Starting and extinguishing fire is not to be done on this day, so all cooking for Sabbath meals is to be done ahead of time. Children are bathed and houses cleaned by late Friday afternoon.

This way, when Sabbath arrives, the stresses of household labors are alleviated, leaving only peaceful and joyous activities for the day.

CANDLES

Nothing quite captures the feeling and excitement of the Jewish holidays like candles.

These are especially important in the ceremony greeting the Sabbath. Many fond childhood memories of growing up in a Jewish home have something in common—watching the candles as blessings are recited. The candles themselves, bright and burning have inspired many poems. One of my favorite is called, "The Light Eternal:"

> Candles aflame and ebb and flicker;
> Shadows dance and die or swell:
> Beams grow brighter, darkness thicker—
> Thus these tapers flash farewell.
>
> But within us have not dwindled
> Sabbath light and Sabbath joy;
> What the candle-beams have kindled
> Death itself cannot destroy.
>
> There are sparks that perish never;
> There are rays death cannot claim;
> In the Jewish heart forever
> Flows the *Torah's* age-long flame (Burstein, 52).

The candle, symbolizing the fervent passion of the Jew, is ever-present in holiday observance.

With a table set with white linen and a beautiful bouquet of flowers, the traditional Jewish home is ready to greet the Sabbath. The candles are usually white, although other colors are becoming more popular. Two candles are used to welcome the Sabbath in a symbolic reference to the two areas in the *Torah* (literally meaning "Instructions" referring to The Five Books of Moses or Pentateuch) where Sabbath observance is commanded.[19] The former tells us that we must *zachor* (remember) the Sabbath, and the latter account tells us to *shamor* (keep) it.

Eighteen minutes before sundown, the Sabbath candles are lit.[20] Why eighteen minutes? The word "life" in Hebrew is *chai*. The letters for *chai* are *chet* and *yod* (חי). These two letters together also make the number eighteen. Therefore, the number eighteen and the word for life are the same. Judaism shows great appreciation for symbolism, and since the Sabbath is a day of life, it is appropriate that we greet it as such.

The actual lighting of the candles calls for the lighter (usually the most senior female in the home) to either sing or say the blessing for the candles. There is a slight alteration to the sequence required here, as the candles are not to be lit after the blessing is sung, as the blessing denotes the onset of Sabbath observance. Remember, creating fire is not to happen after the greeting of the Sabbath in both Biblical and Orthodox Judaism. Also, the candles are not to be enjoyed until after the blessing is said for them. What results is this: the woman will face the candles and light them (usually with her head covered out of respect). She will sweep her hands thrice over the flame as to capture and bring into herself the actual light of the flame. Here is symbolized the welcoming of the light, peace and sanctity of Sabbath into her heart and home. The eyes are closed, or shielded, as the blessing is said, so that the light is not enjoyed prematurely. The traditional blessing for lighting the candles, transliterated from Hebrew, is as follows:

Baruch ata Adonai Eloheinu Melech ha-olam asher kideshanu bemitzvotov vitzivanu lehadlik ner shel Shabbat. (Amen).

---

[19] Exodus 20:8-11; Deuteronomy 5:12-15
[20] Sometimes this tradition varies; in Jerusalem, candles are often lit forty minutes prior to sundown.

In English:

Blessed are You, Lord our God, King of the universe, who has sanctified us with His commandments, and commanded us to kindle the light of the Sabbath. (Amen).

Although the most senior woman of the home is traditionally the candle lighter, it is becoming more common for all female members of the household to share in the privilege (or even males if no females are present). The reasons the women are the ones to light the candles and thereby greet the Sabbath are threefold: 1. women are the tenders of the home, usually, so since it is her domain, she has the honor of lighting the candles; 2., since Eve, by eating the forbidden fruit (and offering it to her husband) extinguished the "candle of God," the woman is therefore allowed to act in atonement for this by lighting the Sabbath candles in an attempt to rekindle the "candle of God;" 3., it is the woman who determines the spiritual nature of the home. She, by promoting the study of scripture, the observance of God's commandments, and creating a nurturing environment, has the power to make the house a place of "holiness, peace and tranquility" (Katz, accessed 12 May 2010). Thus, unless the house is devoid of women, the feminine presence is required for the performance of this mitzvah, or deed.

BLESSING THE FAMILY

The family (*mishpacha*) blessing is one of the most poignant and important parts of greeting the Sabbath. Here, the family is gathered around the Sabbath table. Cell phones are turned off; the television is off; radios and internet are switched off. Here, the only interaction is between the family, friends if present, and God. The male head of the household begins the family blessings by reading a portion of Proverbs 31 known as the passage of "The Wife of Valor" to his wife in appreciation for her and her love and service to the family. Many times, the stresses and obligations of the work week cause us to forget to admonish and edify the ones we love the most and who most need our open and public affirmation. This is a perfect time to lift up each family member.

BLESSING THE WIFE/ MOTHER

The husband turns to his wife and reads the following in dedication to his mate:

> A wife of noble character who can find?
> She is worth far more than rubies.
>
> Her husband has full confidence in her
> and lacks nothing of value.
>
> She brings him good, not harm,
> all the days of her life.
>
> She selects wool and flax
> and works with eager hands.
>
> She is like the merchant ships,
> bringing her food from afar.
>
> She gets up while it is still dark;
> she provides food for her family
> and portions for her servant girls.
>
> She considers a field and buys it;
> out of her earnings she plants a vineyard.
>
> She sets about her work vigorously;
> her arms are strong for her tasks.
>
> She sees that her trading is profitable,
> and her lamp does not go out at night.
>
> In her hand she holds the distaff
> and grasps the spindle with her fingers.

She opens her arms to the poor
and extends her hands to the needy.

When it snows, she has no fear for her household;
for all of them are clothed in scarlet.

She makes coverings for her bed;
she is clothed in fine linen and purple.

Her husband is respected at the city gate,
where he takes his seat among the elders of the land.

She makes linen garments and sells them,
and supplies the merchants with sashes.

She is clothed with strength and dignity;
she can laugh at the days to come.

She speaks with wisdom,
and faithful instruction is on her tongue.

She watches over the affairs of her household
and does not eat the bread of idleness.

Her children arise and call her blessed;
her husband also, and he praises her:

"Many women do noble things,
but you surpass them all."

Charm is deceptive, and beauty is fleeting;
but a woman who fears the LORD is to be praised.

Give her the reward she has earned,
and let her works bring her praise at the city gate.[21]

---

[21] Proverbs 31:10-31

BLESSING THE HUSBAND/ FATHER[22]

This is sure to bring a smile to the face of the wife/ mother of the home, who in like appreciation has the option to bless her husband in like manner:

> **Praise the LORD.**
> **Blessed is the man who fears the LORD,**
> **who finds great delight in his commands.**
>
> **His children will be mighty in the land;**
> **the generation of the upright will be blessed.**
>
> **Wealth and riches are in his house,**
> **and his righteousness endures forever.**
>
> **Even in darkness light dawns for the upright,**
> **for the gracious and compassionate and righteous man.**
>
> **Good will come to him who is generous and lends freely,**
> **who conducts his affairs with justice.**
>
> **Surely he will never be shaken;**
> **a righteous man will be remembered forever.**
>
> **He will have no fear of bad news;**
> **his heart is steadfast, trusting in the LORD.**
>
> **His heart is secure, he will have no fear;**
> **in the end he will look in triumph on his foes.**
>
> **He has scattered abroad his gifts to the poor,**
> **his righteousness endures forever;**
> **his horn will be lifted high in honor.**[23]

---

[22] The blessing of the husband/father is a relatively new addition and does not exist in some jewish traditions.
[23] Psalm 112:1-9

BLESSING THE CHILDREN

The blessing of the children comes next. Hearing a pronunciation of good upon them by their parent(s) is a priceless and incredibly meaningful part of the children's Sabbath-welcoming ceremony of the home. The girls and boys can be blessed separately or together. It is customary to place a hand on their heads as the blessings are recited:

For boys:

May God make you like Ephraim and Manasseh.

For girls:

May God make you like Sarah, Rebekah, Rachel & Leah.

All:

**The Lord bless you
and keep you.
The Lord make His face to shine upon you
And be gracious to you.
The Lord turn His face toward you
and give you peace.**[24]

In analyzing this, we might ask why the boys are to be like Ephraim and Manasseh. Of the myriad of male heroes in the Bible, why would we choose Ephraim and Manasseh over them all? Why prefer them over Moses, Joshua, or even their father Joseph who was full of integrity and God's Spirit? Why not Noah who God trusted with the repopulation of the earth, Abraham who was God's friend, Jacob who was God's servant, David who God loved, Daniel who was faithful, or even the righteous Elijah or Enoch who were both translated to Heaven? What is so special about Ephraim and Manasseh? Of all the children of Jacob (howbeit these were via Joseph), these boys alone were raised in a pagan society.

---

[24] Numbers 6:24-26

Ephraim and Manasseh did not have the luxury of growing to manhood in an environment where the people revered the true God. They were reared in Egypt. Although they grew to manhood in such a notoriously heathen setting, their hearts were nevertheless inclined towards God. They sought righteousness, even though it was considered foolishness by the world. Peer pressure did not sway them. Thus, in blessing our sons to be of such noble character in the midst of ungodliness and corruption, we give them an added measure of strength.

Why do we bless our daughters and extol them to be like Sarah, Rebekah, Rachel and Leah? Why do we not say Jochabed who birthed and raised the hero Moses or even mention the prophetess Miriam his sister? Why not choose Deborah the strong and righteous judge, Jael who killed a king and (in a large part) conquered an enemy nation, or Esther the orphan-turned-queen who saved Israel? Among the four chosen matriarchs, Sarah, Rebekah, Rachel and Leah, were experiences such as the pain of years of barrenness, jealousy, bitterness, hardship, and unrequited love. Despite this, they were steadfast in their faithfulness to their husbands and overcame adversity. They were compassionate, yet their tenacity in triumphing over diverse challenges and obstacles made them role models for future generations. These were also women of promise. An alternate blessing for daughters:

> **[May you be as] Sarah, Rebekah, Rachel, and Leah, the four names recited in the Sabbath blessing on our daughters.**
>
> **May you be beautiful [and beautiful in spirit as was Leah].**
>
> **May you hear from God.**
>
> **May you be fruitful and have children who grow to be men of stature. May you be found faithful even in the midst of struggle**
>
> **May you not forget the Lord and give Him praise in all things.**

> These are the things we wish on our daughters when we bless them with the names of our matriarchs.
>
> All were divinely chosen by God to fulfill His purpose.
>
> All chose to serve the Lord and seek His face to answer their hearts' cry. (Felton, accessed 24 Apr 2010).

Felton ends his discourse with the final question, "what else would we want for our daughters?" The remaining part of the blessing is simply the Aaronic blessing. Alternatively, some have preferred the blessing for daughters from the musical *Fiddler on the Roof*. While it does choose different biblical characters to be role models for the daughters, it still has a beautiful blessing element worthy of any Shabbat table when recited by parents for their daughters.

Parents:

> May the Lord protect and defend you. May He always shield you from shame. May you come to be In Israel a shining name. May you be like Ruth and like Esther. May you be deserving of praise. Strengthen them, Oh Lord, And keep them from the strangers' ways. May God bless you and grant you long lives. (May the Lord fulfill our Sabbath prayer for you.) May God make you good mothers and wives. (May He send you husbands who will care for you.) May the Lord protect and defend you. May the Lord preserve you from pain. Favor them, Oh Lord, with happiness and peace. Oh, hear our Sabbath prayer. (Amen).[25]

This encompasses the children's blessing and leads us into the next part of our Sabbath celebration.

---

[25] Harlick, Sheldon. "Sabbath Prayer" in Fiddler on the Roof.

WINE

The most common sequence of events would next include the onset of *Kiddush*, or the blessing over wine, which denotes the holiness of the day. Wine is biblically used as a symbol of joy.[26] Traditionally, God is blessed for this joyous liquid before it is tasted. The *Kiddush* can be spoken or, like the candle blessing, sung as a song:

> *Baruch Ata Adonai Eloheinu Melech ha-olam boray peri hagafen. (Amen.)*

In English:

> **Blessed are You, Lord our God, King of the universe, Who creates fruit of the vine. (Amen).**

The blessing, of which a short version is listed above,[27] is said while a cup filled with the wine is raised by the right hand (or left if left-handed) with fingers traditionally facing upwards as the base of the cup rests upon the palm (Simcha, accessed 12 May 2010). It is traditional to glance at the Sabbath candles while beginning the blessing and to look upon the wine as the "*borei prei hag-a-fen*" is sung (or said). Every-

---

[26] Non-alcoholic grape juice is a suitable and appropriate substitute for "wine."

[27] The entire Kiddush is longer with English version as follows: "[On] the sixth day... the heavens and the earth and all their hosts were completed. And God finished by the seventh day His work which He had done, and He rested on the seventh day from all His work which He had done. And God blessed the seventh day and made it holy, for on it He rested from all His work which God created to function. Blessed are You, Lord our God, King of the universe, who creates the fruit of the vine. (Amen) Blessed are You, Lord our God, King of the universe, who has hallowed us with His commandments, has desired us, and has given us, in love and goodwill, His holy *Shabbat* as a heritage, in remembrance of the work of Creation; the first of the holy festivals, commemorating the Exodus from Egypt. For You have chosen us and sanctified us from among all the nations, and with love and goodwill given us Your holy *Shabbat* as a heritage. Blessed are You Lord, who hallows the *Shabbat*. (Amen)"

one is then invited to drink of the *Kiddush* wine in celebration of the Sabbath.

Once the wine is sipped, the hands are to be washed. As water symbolizes life and purification, once again the "life" metaphor is used while also offering a practical act of cleanliness. This is done without outside words or distracting conversation. A cup with water is usually poured over the hands while the following blessing is recited:

> ***Baruch atah Adonai, Eloheinu Melech ha-olam, asher kideshanu bemitzvotav vetzivanu al netilat yadayim. (Amen.)***

In English:

> **Blessed are You Lord our God King of the universe Who has sanctified us with His commandments and commanded us concerning the washing of hands. (Amen).**

The hands are now thoroughly dried in anticipation of the sweet bread to come.

BREAD

The *challah*, or sweet egg bread, is now exposed (it is kept covered until this point). Traditionally two braided loaves grace the Sabbath table. The number two is to signify the two portions of manna that God gave to the Jewish people while in the wilderness after escaping from Egypt. The manna had to be gathered on Friday in a double portion to last through the Sabbath, as no manna was to be gathered upon the seventh day.

Jewish culture revolves around many things. Except for the fast days, food and cooking is almost always an important part of the holiday. Sabbath is no different. Preparing and baking *challah* is an important part of the welcoming of the day.

Why *challah* bread? This sweet egg bread is usually a light fluffy white bread made without dairy and braided. Sometimes poppy or sesame seeds adorn the top. On holidays, or whenever preferred, raisins and small pieces of dried fruit can be added to make a type of light fruit bread. Although Jews worldwide enjoy the honey-sweetened *challah* egg bread, it was especially enjoyed in Eastern Europe. With heavy pumpernickel-type breads the staple, a light sweet *challah* was an anticipated celebratory morsel for welcoming the Sabbath, a tasty and aesthetically golden treat on the table.

Where does the idea of *challah* come from? Many believe it originated in Eastern Europe because of its popularity there, however its roots are much deeper—four thousand years deeper! The tradition of baking a weekly leavened bread, the *challah*, actually originated in scripture with instructions given to Moses regarding the building, upkeep and observances of the Tabernacle:

> You shall take choice flour and bake of it twelve loaves, tow-tenths of a measure for each loaf. Place them on the pure table before the LORD in two rows, six to a row.... He shall arrange them before the LORD regularly every Sabbath day— it is a commitment for all time on the part of the Israelites.[28]

Commonly also known as shewbread (or sometimes spelled "showbread"), this bread is the founding father of the modern golden *challah*, the focus of the *Shabbat* table. This is a very enjoyable and tasty part of the celebration! The *Ha-Motzi* blessing is said over the bread as follows:

Baruch ata Adonai, Eloheinu Melech ha-olam, ha-motzi lechem min ha-aretz. (Amen.)

In English:

Blessed are You Lord our God, King of the universe, Who brings forth bread of the earth. (Amen).

---

[28] Leviticus 24:5-8

The bread is then broken or cut and distributed to all the family members. It is also customary to dip the bread in salt before eating. (This is a reminder of the salt offered with every Temple sacrifice).[29] The bread is then eaten and enjoyed, followed by the Sabbath meal. Charity, or *tzedakah*, is an important part of Sabbath as well as most all Jewish holidays. A box usually is sitting by with donations for the less fortunate, although the money itself is not touched during the Sabbath hours.

This traditional welcoming of the Sabbath is likened to a groom's gleeful anticipation of his beautiful bride. The whole family is to eagerly await the Sabbath as a wedding celebration. The Sabbath is also referred to as *Shabbat Hamalka*, the Sabbath Queen, as there are also rules to be obeyed concerning the Sabbath.

SONGS

The Sabbath table is also a place for songs to be sung together. The classic is *Shalom Aleichem* and is sung in most Jewish homes on the onset of the Sabbath. It is sung in reference to the angels present upon the greeting of the Sabbath. The lyrics are as follows:

> *Shalom Aleichem malachei hasharet malachei elyon.*
> *Mimelech malachei ham lachim hakadosh baruch Hu.*
>
> *Bo-achem leshalom malachei hashalom malachei elyon*
> *Mimelech malachei hamlachim hakadosh baruch Hu.*
>
> *Barchuni leshalom mal'achei hashalom mal'achei elyon*
> *Mimelech malachei ham lachim hakadosh baruch Hu.*
>
> *Tzetchem leshalom mal'achei hashalom malachei elyon*
> *Mimelech malachei ham lachim hakadosh baruch Hu.*

---

[29] Leviticus 2:13

In English:

Peace upon you, ministering angels, messengers of the Most High, of the Supreme King of Kings, the Holy One, blessed be He.

Come in peace, messengers of peace, messengers of the Most High, of the Supreme King of Kings, the Holy One, blessed be He.

Bless me with peace, messengers of peace, messengers of the Most High, of the Supreme King of Kings, the Holy One, blessed be He.

May your departure be in peace, messengers of peace, messengers of the Most High, of the Supreme King of Kings, the Holy One, blessed be He.

Some children songs are also used, such as the very popular *"Bim Bom (Shabbat Shalom)"*:

**Bim bom, bim bim bim bom, bim bim bim bim bim bom,
Shabbat shalom hey! *Shabbat shalom* hey!
Shabbat Shabbat Shabbat, Shabbat shalom!** (repeat)[30]

At this point, Sabbath dinner commences with all of the weekday concerns forgotten, with all the stress and worry of daily business left outside of the perimeter of the home.

SEPARATION (HAVDALAH): THE CLOSE OF THE SABBATH

The Sabbath day has been greeted and celebrated. It has been both a delight and a rest. The time then comes for its close. The Sabbath is

---

[30] For tunes, search the Internet for videos under respective titles.

considered past and safely acknowledged as such when three stars are seen in the night sky. Determining when to bid farewell to the Sabbath at "sundown" is not always accurately done by judging the position of the sun, as the actual moment of dusk is often indiscernible. Instead, waiting until at least three stars are visible ensures that the sun is indeed down. This might be difficult to ascertain on cloudy nights, but with clear skies, this is most reliable.

Once Sabbath is confirmed to be over, the Separation (*Havdalah*) ceremony can begin. This is the commemoration that marks the border between the sacred time and the secular. The hallowed Sabbath has ended, and we must go back to the work week. We are leaving the spiritual realm to once again immerse ourselves in the physical material world.

Many great events have a designated opening and a closing. The Olympic Games have an opening and a closing ceremony with special traditions and activities. The celebrated Sabbath should be no less. This ritual, employing all five senses, is just as well an experience as much as an illustration. It is just as enjoyable for the adults as for the children. *Havdalah* hereby prepares us to once again face the work week while carrying the blessings and peace of Sabbath with us.

TEXTS

First, texts are read or recited. These are scriptures to uplift the mind and heart, reminding us of God's power as the source of our salvation. For, although we are losing the Sabbath peace for the week, we do not need to be downhearted or downtrodden, as God's triumph is ours; His blessing goes with us for the week ahead:

> ***Hinay, El yishuati evtach velo efchad, ki azi vezimrat Yah, Adonai, va-yehi li lishu'a.***
> **Surely God is my salvation. I will trust and not be afraid. The LORD, the LORD, is my strength and my song; he has become my salvation.**

Ushe avtem mayim besason, mima-a-yenay ha-yeshua.
With joy you will draw water from the wells of salvation.[31]

La Adonai ha-yeshu'a, al amcha virchatecha, Selah.
From the LORD comes deliverance. May your blessing be on your people. Selah.[32]

Adonai Tzevaot imanu, misgav lanu, Elohay Ya-akov, Selah.
The LORD Almighty is with us; the God of Jacob is our fortress. Selah.[33]

Adonai Tzevaot, ashray adam botayach bach
O LORD Almighty, blessed is the man who trusts in you.[34]

Adonai hoshiah, hamelech ya-anaynu veyom koraynu.
Save, O LORD; may the King answer us in the day we call.[35]

La yehudim hayetah orah vesimcha vesason vikar,
For the Jews it was a time of happiness and joy, gladness and honor.[36]

kayn tehiyeh lanu.
may we have the same.

Kos yeshuot esa uveshaym Adonai Ekra.
I will lift up the cup of salvation and call on the name of the LORD.[37]

---

[31] Isaiah 12:3
[32] Psalm 3:8
[33] Psalm 46:11
[34] Psalm 84:12
[35] Psalm 20:9 NASB
[36] Esther 8:16
[37] Psalm 116:13

WINE

This last text about raising the cup of salvation can be an appropriate usher for the next event of blessing and drinking the wine (or other liquid). This is an interesting part of the ceremony in that the wine is deliberately overflowed and spilled onto the tray beneath the cup as it is poured. This may seem like an accident, but it, like all the traditions of Judaism, is laden with symbolism. Our hearts overflow with joy over the Sabbath, and this joy is to get us through the remainder of the week. The overflowing of the wine here captures this sentiment. With the same blessing used earlier for the *Kiddush*, the wine can be blessed. If using a liquid other than wine, substitute the following blessing:

> *Baruch ata Adonai Eloheinu Melech ha-olam shehakol nihyeh bidvaro. (Amen.)*

In English:

> **Blessed are you Lord God King of the universe Who made all things exist through His word. (Amen).**

SPICES (B'SAMIM)

The spices come next. This is usually comprised of a *b'samim* box (spice holder) with cloves, cinnamon, bay leaves, dried citrus peel and/or another aromatic spice.[38] These fragrant spices are to remind us of the sweetness of Sabbath and are a compensation for the loss of it. The smell of the fragrant spices also lingers as does the beautiful peace of Sabbath. When we are around a strong aroma, that aroma clings to us. In the same manner, it is our hope that the sweet peace of Sabbath lingers with us and goes with us to our respective work places during the days of the week. The blessing is said before passing the spices around:

---

[38] The citron, or *etrog*, of *Sukkot* can be used as will be explained later.

Baruch ata Adonai Eloheinu Melech ha-olam boray minay vesamin. (Amen.)

In English:

Blessed are You, Lord our God, King of the universe, Who creates the fruit of the vine. (Amen).

FIRE (AYSH)

Next comes the torch, or the *Havdalah* candle. This is a candle with six wicks or is comprised of six slim candles woven into one resembling a braid. Each wick symbolizes a work day, although a candle with more than one wick can be used if one with six is not available. If even this is difficult to come by, it is commonly understood as permissible to hold two regular candles together so that their wicks are close enough to make one flame between the two. Now comes the lighting of the candle(s). Jewish tradition, as per Rabbi Yehudah in the Talmud, holds that fire is significant for *Havdalah*, as not only was light the first element created by God, but fire itself was said to have been made at the conclusion of the first Sabbath in Eden.[39] Often, it is customary to look at the back of our hand as we recite the blessing, symbolizing that now we are dealing with the superficial outer world once again, as the hidden sacred world (represented by the inside of the hand) is once again hidden until the Sabbath returns. Also, while reciting the blessing, we enjoy the flame; we curl our fingers over and near it, noting the reflection of the light on our fingernails and the shadows cast upon our palm. (In Judaism, it is silly to recite a blessing over something and not enjoy it!) The blessing is as follows:

Baruch ata Adonai Eloheinu Melech ha-olam, boray meoray ha-aysh. (Amen.)

---

[39] Pesahim 53:b

In English:

Blessed are you Lord God, King of the Universe, Creator of the fire's light. (Amen).

The candle light is enjoyed to its fullest if the room is otherwise darkened. Seeing the candle's glow in the faces of the family is a beautiful part of this tradition. Also, the extinguishing of the candle later at the end of the ceremony is all the more dramatic when the room's sole light source is this candle light. The final blessing is then said over the wine.

SEPARATION BLESSING (HAVDALAH BRACHAH)

The final blessing is the *Havdalah* blessing itself. This blessing is said over the wine which is finally drunk after this blessing:

Baruch ata Adonai, Eloheinu, melekh ha-olam
hamavdil bein kodesh lechol
bein or lechoshekh bein Yisrael la-amim
bein yom hashvi'i lesheishet yemei hama-aseh
Barukh ata Adonai, hamavdil bein kodesh lechol (Amen).

In English:

Blessed are you, Lord, our God, sovereign of the universe
Who separates between sacred and secular
between light and darkness, between Israel and the nations
between the seventh day and the six days of labor
Blessed are You, Lord, who separates between sacred and secular. (Amen)

After the blessing and the drinking of the wine, the candle is extinguished. This is done by dousing the flame into the spilled puddle of wine left over from the overflow of the cup when it was first filled. The *pfft* of the dying flame renders the room in darkness. The Sabbath is over, and we are left in the darkness of the work week until we can greet the sacred day once more. At this point, it is our family's tradition to have someone (who has been previously posted near the light switch) turn on the light, so that when the *havdalah* flame is out, we do not fumble around in the pitch-black darkness. After a pregnant pause, a poignant silence in the dark after losing the light of the Sabbath as well as the light of the candle, the room's light-switch is turned on. Upon the lighting of the room once more, we shout in unison, "*shavua tov*" (literally Hebrew for "have a good week"). We will need this joy to bring us through the week until we are blessed with the return of Sabbath once more.

This rich *Havdalah* tradition invites all of the five senses to participation. The light of the flame can be both seen and felt—two of the senses engaged. The wine is tasted. The spices are smelled. The texts which began the ceremony ring in the ears. All the senses are thus stimulated for this closing ceremony of the holy Sabbath, so even children cannot help but pay attention and remember. The secular next six days are reluctantly ushered in with a hope and prayer that the remembrance of Sabbath peace will follow us and get us through the week ahead.

JESUS AND SABBATH (YESHUA AND SHABBAT)

Yeshua is very connected to the Sabbath by not only his example of miracles he performs on the day, but also by his own admission. Scripture states, "Then Yeshua said to them, 'The Son of Man is Lord of the Sabbath.'"[40] Yeshua always acted in accordance with the divine Sabbath commandment, both scripturally as well as rabbinically. Some argue that he broke the rabbinical interpretation of the Sabbath laws, but this is not the case. For example, Yeshua was accused of breaking a Sabbath law when he placed his hands upon a deformed, crippled woman and healed her.[41] Although this and other healings are often portrayed to have

---

[40] Luke 6:5
[41] Luke 13:10-17

clashed with the Jewish laws of the time, they were in actuality in accordance with the laws and were permitted by Tannaitic Law. He observed the Sabbath closely and *in like manner* as the other leaders of the day. So, in Yeshua's healing upon the Sabbath, the law is fulfilled in graciousness while not being abolished or in any way severed [nor even challenged in its rabbinical interpretation]. After all, he reminds, humanity was not made for the Sabbath, but Sabbath was made for humanity.[42]

Why is Sabbath important? Why is our Messiah the Lord of the Sabbath? Sabbath will be finally manifest in its final and truest form during the reign of Yeshua after his return to earth. This millennial rule of the Messiah, known as the "World to Come" in Jewish tradition is likened to the Peaceable Kingdom:

> *A shoot will come up from the stump of Jesse;*
> *from his roots a Branch will bear fruit.*
>
> *The Spirit of the LORD will rest on him—*
> *the Spirit of wisdom and of understanding,*
> *the Spirit of counsel and of power,*
> *the Spirit of knowledge and of the fear of the LORD –*
>
> *And he will delight in the fear of the LORD....*
>
> *Righteousness will be his belt*
> *and faithfulness the sash around his waist.*
>
> *The wolf will live with the lamb,*
> *the leopard will lie down with the goat,*
> *the calf and the lion and the yearling together;*
>
> *And a little child will lead them....*
>
> *They will neither harm nor destroy*
> *on all my holy mountain,*

---

[42] Mark 2:27

*for the earth will be full of the knowledge of the LORD
as the waters cover the sea.*

*In that day the Root of Jesse will stand as a banner for the
peoples; the nations will rally to him, and his place of rest
will be glorious.*[43]

This "Great Sabbath" will be marked by peace and harmony. Today's Sabbath is to be but a glimpse of this blissful time to come, the age foretold. Since our weekly Sabbath is a foreshadowing of this future event, this is not just for Jews but for all the followers of God who anticipate such a time.

Yeshua is present in the symbol of the wine. I am not talking about the obvious Christian understanding of Eucharist, or the wine as "the blood of Jesus," or even as the joy (all very valid connections with Yeshua), but, importantly, I am discussing the link between the symbol of the wine and the manifest kingship of our Messiah. Each time we sing the blessing over the wine, we are saying a blessing to our divine "King of the Universe" Who "creates the fruit of the vine." From this basic and perhaps most oft-recited blessing, we can know and affirm the Divine King of the Universe that brings forth the wine that we sing over. When greeting the Sabbath or partaking of the *Kiddush*, the wine is usually the first thing blessed and consumed. This brings us to analyze the significance of another "first"—the first miracle of Yeshua. I have often heard the question of why Yeshua's first recorded miracle was one of turning water to wine—such a seemingly frivolous or trivial task for a miracle worker. When we bring the idea of "wine preceding all else" in the chronological order of service, and we take into account its blessing affirming "the King of the Universe Who [alone] creates the fruit of the vine," we can see that *this first miracle was nothing less than an affirmation of divine Kingship*—for Yeshua, in creating wine, did what *only* the King of the Universe could. He "created the fruit of the vine."

---

[43] Isaiah 11:1-10

Yeshua is also reflected in the symbol of the *challah* bread. While the body of the Messiah is never represented by using leavened bread; we must look at the role that the bread itself plays. Most Christians metaphorically describe Yeshua as being the "Bread of life." He is often compared to bread, having even been born in *Bethlehem*, literally defined as the "City of Bread." Bread sustains us, leavened or not. Bread has been the principle player in the Middle Eastern diet; it has been a staple of the people of the Bible for millennia.

What is the purpose of the showbread in the Tabernacle or Temple if God is not going to eat it? The *challah* and the table it laid on were both symbols of fellowship. The idea of God dining with man is a concept of intimacy. Especially in the Middle East, dining together is a vital part of a friendship or even an acquaintance. For many, even business transactions often must take place over a meal. God is definitely a supreme and awesome God, yet He is not so far removed in all of his glory to forsake the company of humanity. This table and its presentation of bread, the staple diet of the biblical culture, denote that God is inviting humanity to commune with Him.

Yeshua further fulfills the emblem of the showbread, *challah*, by exemplifying God's plan to dwell among humanity. Choosing to walk this dark and sinful world after leaving the glory and bliss of Heaven, Yeshua dwelt, fellowshipped and communed with fallen humanity. Like the *challah* prepared and baked for the Tabernacle each week, representing the communal joy of togetherness, Yeshua came to dwell with us, cleansing us from our sins so that we may enter the true "rest" of God's kingdom.

HOW CAN THIS BENEFIT YOU, A CHRISTIAN?

One does not have to be Jewish to enjoy the sanctity of the seventh-day Sabbath, the crowning day of creation. Since the creation of humankind (not just Jewish-kind), God has set aside this special time as holy. He rested on this day Himself in a divine example of cherishing the day. In a very physical sense, resting and observing this day as one of repose provides healing for everyone physically, emotionally, psychologically and spiritually. Since even the animals are to be spared work in honor of this day, how much more should all of humanity benefit?

The Sabbath is not just Jewish, as it is God's day—this same God of the Christian as of the Jew. Therefore, we are not simply to rest, but to rest *in Him*. Simply lounging around in pajamas does not necessarily capture the true spirit of the day. During the six workdays of the week, we are immersed in the physical world around us. Things change on Sabbath. On this holy, day, we are instead involved with the spiritual world. On the six days of the work week, we are in the office, administrative buildings or marketplace; on Sabbath, we are spending time with God and family. Sabbath is a day for introspection. We have this time especially for communing with God and taking stock of our spirituality.

We are described by Rabbi Yaacov Hillel as being both spiritual and physical in nature. When one side is expanded and developed, the other side diminishes. One side dominates; the other side submits. As we build up our spiritual side, our physical will lose it power over us. However, the opposite is also true, if we empower the physical side and make it most important in our lives, our spiritual side may suffer neglect. The Sabbath helps us gain a balance. Six days a week find us in the secular world working for our living. Even if we are doing holy things during this time and praying regularly, we are still in the physical mode. On Sabbath, all this is halted. The spiritual side is then allowed to rise up to higher levels. We rest on the Sabbath and delve deeper into the spiritual world (Hillel, accessed 25 Apr 2010).

Sabbath provides for us a little slice of heaven. The Bible tells us that the Sabbath is to be an actual delight! With every abstaining "no," there is a joyous "yes" as well. When we take away a secular bit of fun from the day, we replace that with a spiritual treat or special joy or element of celebration! The opportunities are endless: worship together, visit the elderly and lonely with singing and smiles. Bring in some new tradition, family time and maybe even outdoor adventures (for the high energy types) all in the aim of spiritual recuperation that is tailored to suit your family. We can imagine putting down a heavy backpack. The weightless sensation on our shoulders would be so welcome and refreshing. This is the comforting feeling of the Sabbath. We lay down our cares of the outside world and soak up the joy and love of family and God. This is our spiritual battery recharging time! Anyone can benefit from such joys of the Sabbath. Everyone can use such a refresher!

HOLIDAY NOSHES (SNACKS)

Enjoy the *challah* tradition with the easy recipe. Remember to always make two loaves. The aroma of baking *challah* is a wonderful way to get yourself and family into the mode of welcoming the Sabbath.

EASY CHALLAH (pareve—non-dairy, non-meat)

Ingredients

- 1 (.25 ounce) package active dry yeast
- 1 cup warm water (100 degrees F)
- 2-4 tablespoons honey (depending upon desired sweetness)
- 1 teaspoon salt
- 3 beaten eggs (ensure no blood spots)
- 3 1/2 cups all-purpose flour, plus more for kneading

Variation

- Add 1 tablespoon oil to dough before/while kneading
- For golden creamy-colored bread, steep a pinch of saffron for 10 minutes in boiling water. Remove saffron. Let water cool somewhat and use as the cup of "warm" water in the recipe.

Directions

1. In a large bowl, stir the yeast into the water, and let the mixture stand until a creamy layer forms on top, about 10 minutes. Stir in honey and salt until dissolved, and add the beaten eggs. Mix in the flour, a cupful at a time, until the dough is sticky. Place dough on floured surface, and knead until smooth and elastic, about 5 minutes.

2. Form the dough into a ball, and place in an oiled bowl. Turn the dough over several times in the bowl to oil the surface of the dough, cover the bowl with a warm damp cloth, and let rise in a warm area until doubled in size, 45 minutes to 1 hour.

3. Punch down the dough, and cut it into 6 equal-sized pieces. Working on a floured surface, roll the small dough pieces into ropes about the thickness of your thumb and about 12 inches long. Ropes should be thicker in the middle and thinner at the ends. Pinch 3 ropes together at the top and braid them. Starting with the strand to the right, move it to the left over the middle strand (that strand becomes the new middle strand.) Take the strand farthest to the left, and move it over the new middle strand. Continue braiding, alternating sides each time, until the 2 loaves are braided, and pinch the ends together and fold under for a neat look.

4. Place the braided loaf on a parchment-lined baking sheet lined with parchment paper, and brush the top with beaten egg. (For a softer crust, brush with oil instead. However, if a crispier crust is desired, place a pan of water in the oven while baking).

5. Preheat oven to 350 F.

6. Bake the *challah* in the preheated oven until the top browns to a rich golden color and the loaf sounds hollow when you tap it with a spoon, 30 to 35 minutes. Cool on a wire rack before slicing.

7. ENJOY!

Matzah balls are a great part of a Sabbath meal. These are great simmered in your favorite broth—chicken flavored, onion, mushroom or vegetable. This recipe makes a half dozen golf-ball-sized balls (I often make them smaller to yield a full twelve).

MATZAH BALLS (pareve)

Ingredients

- 2 large eggs, beaten lightly
- 3/4 cup *matzah* meal (or very finely crumbled *matzah* crackers)
- 1/8 cup margarine
- 1 teaspoon salt or powdered broth flavoring/ soup mix (use 2 if boiled in bland broth)
- 1/8 cup hot water
- 4 or more cups of salted broth (chicken flavor, onion, or vegetable)

Directions

1. In a medium bowl, mix the eggs and margarine together.
2. Stir in *matzah* meal and salt.
3. Add hot water.
4. Mix well. Let stand for 15 minutes.
5. With oiled hands, form balls approximately golf ball size or 1 1/2 inches in diameter. (Add more liquid if dough is not moist enough, or add more meal if too moist).
6. Carefully drop balls into boiling broth. Cook 15 minutes on a medium boil.
7. ENJOY!

PASSOVER (PESACH)

On the Jewish calendar: 15 *Nissan* (March-April)

Observe the month of Abib[44] and celebrate the Passover of the LORD your God, because in the month of Abib he brought you out of Egypt by night. Sacrifice as the Passover to the LORD your God an animal from your flock or herd at the place the LORD will choose as a dwelling for his Name. Do not eat it with bread made with yeast, but for seven days eat unleavened bread, the bread of affliction, because you left Egypt in haste—so that all the days of your life you may remember the time of your departure from Egypt. Let no yeast be found in your possession in all your land for seven days. Do not let any of the meat you sacrifice on the evening of the first day remain until morning.[45]

HOLIDAY BACKGROUND

What is the Passover? The Passover is explained in a story that retells the beginning of Israel's story in Egypt began with the arrival of Joseph after he was sold as a slave by his brothers. He was taken to Egypt where, after

---

[44] Or *Aviv* also known as *Nissan*
[45] Deuteronomy 16:1-4

the hardship of slavery and even prison, he was elevated to a position over all of Egypt except for Pharaoh himself. During the time of famine, his family came to get food from Egypt. Because of Joseph, their needs were met, and thus they remained in Egypt. All these children of Jacob, or Israel, began to multiply.

Four generations later, they were so prolific that the current Pharaoh felt they were a threat to his kingdom. Scripture says that this ruler did not know Joseph, from which we can deduct that he may very well have known *of* him but did not embrace him or *know* him as the intimate biblical usage of the word implies. By this time, Israel had become slaves and were not allowed the freedom to worship and sacrifice to God. Pharaoh finally sought horrific, yet ultimately futile, measures such as infanticide to control the increasing numbers of the Israelites.

Despite the infanticide decree to extinguish the life of all males, one was spared and became adopted by the very daughter of Pharaoh. This child was the famous leader of the nation who ultimately led Israel into her own nationhood and to the border of the Promised Land. He was Moses.

Moses demanded, through God's authority, that Pharaoh let Israel leave so that they may be free to worship God. Pharaoh did not let the slaves free as God demanded, so God brought plagues upon both him and the Egyptian people. After a barrage of frogs, lice, beasts (some interpret these as flies), diseased livestock, boils, fiery hailstones, locusts, and darkness hit the land, Pharaoh still refused. Finally, as Pharaoh was still stubbornly preventing the Jewish slaves to go free, the final plague was brought upon him and all of his Egyptians. God gave specific instructions to Moses:

> ***Tell the whole community of Israel that on the tenth day of this month each man is to take a lamb for his family, one for each household. If any household is too small for a whole lamb, they must share one with their nearest neighbor, having taken into account the number of people there are. You***

are to determine the amount of lamb needed in accordance with what each person will eat. The animals you choose must be year-old males without defect, and you may take them from the sheep or the goats. Take care of them until the fourteenth day of the month, when all the people of the community of Israel must slaughter them at twilight. Then they are to take some of the blood and put it on the sides and tops of the doorframes of the houses where they eat the lambs. That same night they are to eat the meat roasted over the fire, along with bitter herbs, and bread made without yeast. Do not eat the meat raw or cooked in water, but roast it over the fire—head, legs and inner parts. Do not leave any of it till morning; if some is left till morning, you must burn it. This is how you are to eat it: with your cloak tucked into your belt, your sandals on your feet and your staff in your hand. Eat it in haste; it is the LORD's Passover. On that same night I will pass through Egypt and strike down every firstborn—both men and animals—and I will bring judgment on all the gods of Egypt. I am the LORD.[46]

Thus, with these instructions, the Jewish people experienced their first Passover—literally, the "passing over" of the Divine hand bringing death to the firstborn. With the blood of the lamb smeared on the posts of their houses, they were spared from the wrath of God who took the lives of the Egyptian firstborn that night. This final plague, and survival of the Jewish firstborn, marked the Passover. From here, Pharaoh let the Jewish people go (until he changed his mind and unsuccessfully tried to bring them back), and the great exodus from Egypt commenced; the nation of Israel began to take on a new identity.

Thus, one of the greatest moments in Jewish history was the deliverance from Egyptian slavery for the purpose of worshipping God freely.

---

[46] Exodus 12:3-12

This is forever commemorated by the festival week known as Passover, in reference to the Passover lamb whose blood saved the eldest of each family during the tenth and final plague of Egypt. This holiday encompasses the freedom from not only death but slavery as well. This festival, an old tradition spanning well over three thousand years,[47] includes more than simply the escape from Egypt and Pharaoh, as it has come to include also the liberation from all the threats to the Jewish people and their culture.

> That the beliefs, practices, and sense of peoplehood have survived in complete dispersion for over thousands of years, despite all odds—including pharaohs, czars, kings, Hamans, and Hitlers of every variety—is nothing short of miraculous. Thus, at Passover, we celebrate a freedom we have repeatedly fought to maintain at all costs at all times in all generations (Cordoza, 124).

Passover is the foremost of the festivals which thus causes its month of *Nissan* to be first on the calendar. It was the first national religious holiday of the people, observed even before the Sabbath was re-instituted at Sinai. It was also one of the pilgrimage holidays.

TRADITIONAL OBSERVANCE

Before Passover, a thorough cleaning of the home takes place. All crumbs and dust that can contain yeast particles are swept away in obedience to God's mandate that all leaven be put away from the borders of the home. After thorough cleaning, often a parent will give a child a feather for which to "sweep" any missed leaven up with. Often the parent may hide something leavened, such as a piece of bread, so that the child can find it and enjoy the exercise of removing and disposing of it. More of this is explained later in the section "Feast of Unleavened Bread," as it

---

[47] Some scholars claim *Pesach*, or Passover, was related to an earlier spring festival that existed among nomadic farming Israelites predating the Egyptian slavery correlation.

is ultimately for that holiday for which the house is "sterilized" from yeast. For the actual Passover dinner, *tzedakah*, or charity, is exercised by inviting the less fortunate to both dine together and participate in the celebration of the *seder*.

THE ORDER (SEDER)

The actual *seder* dinner of Passover is in order of the Exodus story and is led by a book, called "The Telling," (the *Haggadah*). This meal features a *seder* of important symbolic edible components.[48] They are as follows:

1. **Bitter Herbs** (*Maror*). This is usually horseradish but sometimes has been bitter lettuce. This represents the bitterness of the hardship of slavery.
2. **Shank Bone of a Lamb** (*Z'roa*). This symbolizes the lamb that the Jews ate hastily before fleeing Egypt.
3. **Unleavened Bread** (*Matzah*). This is made with no leaven and with kosher-for-Passover flour that has not been previously moist (even as wheat) or otherwise allowed to harbor leaven within it. These three ingredients were specified to be eaten ceremoniously.

---

[48] An orange is also sometimes present at modern *seder* dinners. This is a controversial, unconventional, unbiblical, as well as unofficial, addition—but is not necessarily "wrong" to do. It has been adopted as more of a political statement of solidarity and support of women's leadership than anything else. The urban legend states that in the 1980's, a prominent rabbi denounced women as religious leaders during a speech by Susannah Heschel. He supposedly said that a woman had as much place on the *bima* (synagogue platform) as an orange did on a *seder* plate! Ever since then, some have adopted this tradition in support of women's religious leadership rights. I have noticed a conspicuous orange added as a tongue-in-cheek reply to this rabbi's decree placed on quite a few *seder* plates in private homes I have visited for Passover. I mention it so that just in case you see it on someone's *seder* plate, you know now why.

Later, the following items were also added to the *seder* plate:

4. **Bitter Greens** *(Karpas)*. Usually parsley or celery, this is a symbol of spring as well as new life for the nation of Israel. It also represents the hyssop used to sprinkle the blood of the lamb upon the door posts. During the *seder*, this is dipped in salt water to symbolize the tears of pain and anguish of bondage and slavery.

5. **Egg** *(Beitzah)*. This symbolizes new beginnings. By the first Passover, the nation of Israel had already begun to experience for herself the freedom of being a sizable nation for the first time, sanctified and set apart unto their God.

6. **Apple-nut Mixture** *(Charoset)*. This mixture of apples, nuts, wine or juice, raisins and cinnamon (see recipe to follow) is a representation of the mortar used by the Israelite slaves in building the Egyptian monuments. It also is sweet, representing a sweeter life of freedom and following God.

KOSHER WINE / GRAPE JUICE [49]

During the *seder* dinner, it is customary to drink four cups of wine or grape juice. These are to represent the four ways redemption is expressed in the following scripture:

> *Therefore, say to the Israelites: "I am the LORD, and I will <u>bring</u> you out from under the yoke of the Egyptians. I will free [or <u>deliver</u>] you from being slaves to them, and I will <u>redeem</u> you with an outstretched arm and with mighty acts of judgment. I will <u>take</u> you as my own people, and I*

---

[49] "Kosher wine" is officially wine that has been under the supervision of select Jewish authorities during the entire process from grape being picked from the vine to its delivery to the distributor to ensure that it has not come into any contact with yeast or, as was more of a concern in times past, pagan ritual.

will be your God. Then you will know that I am the LORD your God, who brought you out from under the yoke of the Egyptians.[50]

Thus, the first cup is called the cup of sanctification (as in God *brought* them out of Egypt). The second cup is the cup of judgment (as God judged Egypt and *delivered* Israel from her). The third cup is the cup of redemption (as Israel was *redeemed* with an outstretched arm, as the text says quite similarly). The fourth cup is the cup of the kingdom (representing the new kingdom, or Messianic peaceable kingdom to come and to which God will take us). These four cups are always present on Passover regardless of the arrangement of the *haggadah*. The fifth cup later added was to represent Elijah, as Elijah never died but was translated to Heaven alive. During the *seder*, it is customary for a child to open the door to check for Elijah's arrival. Elijah is expected to arrive during the Passover time, some say. Elijah is known as a figure to herald the arrival of the Messiah. John the Baptist was a prophet in the manner of Elijah in preparing the way for Yeshua on earth during his First Coming. Some eschatologists also note that Elijah may also be considered one of the witnesses announcing the Second Coming of Yeshua.

THE HAGGADAH

The actual Passover meal is embedded in the *Seder* ceremony. Following the story, or the *haggadah*, the participants are guided along a symbolic journey to re-experience their liberation from slavery and death to freedom and life. A Passover *haggadah* can be found online or at select religious book centers. They range from traditional Jewish versions to Messianic Jewish ones which will include the Messianic significance of the Passover symbols. The latter are often used at Christian celebrations of the Passover ceremony.

---

[50] Exodus 6:6-7. Emphasis added.

Passover occurs on a specific day. Some Christians, who honestly fancy themselves to be Jewish, celebrate Passover on any spring day that is convenient. This goes against the basic understanding of Jewish holidays when the actual (not approximate) time of year is sacred. Passover is not like a Christmas dinner party that can be celebrated on any day in the season.

Before celebrating Passover, the house must be cleansed from all yeast or *chametz*, as stated earlier. This is followed by the lighting of the candles (see above). Here is a basic list of items used for a *seder* celebration:

- **Holiday candles** (at least two)
- **Carafe of wine or grape juice**
- ***Seder* plate** (or dish with divided areas to isolate each of the six *seder* items

    1. bitter herbs such as horseradish
    2. shankbone of a lamb or suitable equivalent[51]
    3. *matzah*
    4. bitter greens (often romaine lettuce)
    5. roasted egg (in the shell)
    6. apple-nut mixture of *charoset*

- **Cup for Elijah** (some also add **Miriam's Cup**)
- **Three *matzot*,** covered
- ***Afikomen* bag** (or napkin to hide it in)
- **Pillows** for reclining
- **Salt water** for dipping
- **Empty chair** to symbolize those who are not free to celebrate (optional)

---

[51] Vegetarians often use an avocado pit or beetroot to symbolize the lamb bone.

- **Cup, basin and towel** for washing hands
- **Flowers** (optional)
- A copy of **the program, or *haggadah*** for each person
- **Drinking cup** for each person

Following here is a basic order of service. Since "*seder*" is translated to mean "order," we can say, "here is the *seder* of the *seder*."[52]

---

[52] This is a brief example and is not intended to replace an actual *haggadah*

A GENERAL SEDER OF THE PASSOVER SERVICE

Before officially starting the *seder*, it is customary to light the candles (traditionally two as in *Shabbat*) and before gazing up on them, a participant (female if possible), recites the following:

Baruch ata Adonai, Eloheinu Melech ha-olam, asher kideshanu bemitzvotav vetzivanu lehadlik ner shel Yom Tov. (Amen)[53]

In English:

Blessed are You Lord our God, King of the universe, Who has sanctified us with His commandments and commanded us to kindle the festival lights. (Amen).

Follow this with the *Shehecheyanu* blessing:

Baruch ata Adonai, Eloheinu Melech ha-olam, shehecheyanu vekiyenamu, vehigianu la'zeman hazeh. (Amen).

---

[53] On Shabbat, say: "Baruch ata Adonai, Eloheinu Melech ha-olam, asher kideshanu bemitzvotav vetzivanu lehadlik ner shell, Shabbat v'shel Yom Tov." (…to kindle the Sabbath and festival lights.)

In English:

Blessed are You Lord our God, King of the universe, Who gave us life, and sustains us, and enabled us to reach this season of joy. (Amen).

1. <u>*Kadesh*</u> (Blessing and drinking the first cup of wine)
All cups are filled with wine or juice as the following blessing is recited:

Baruch ata Adonai, Eloheinu Melech ha-olam, boray peri hagafen. (Amen).

In English:

Blessed are You, Lord our God, King of the universe, Who creates the fruit of the vine. (Amen).

Together, everyone drinks from their cups.

2. <u>*Urchatz*</u> (Washing our hands)
At a sink or over a basin, take a cup or pitcher in one hand and pour the water over the other hand. Then, switch hands, and repeat. Each person washes his or her own hands silently. No blessing is said at this time.

3. <u>*Karpas*</u> (Dipping a vegetable with a blessing)
Everyone holds and dips a green vegetable, such as parsley, into the salt water and recites the following blessing:

Baruch ata Adonai, Eloheinu Melech ha-olam, boray peri ha-adama. (Amen).

In English:

Blessed are You, Lord our God, King of the universe, who created fruit of the earth. (Amen).

4. *Yachatz* (Breaking the middle *matzah* and hiding the *Afikomen*)
Three covered *matzot* are on the table. The middle one is taken out and broken. The larger half is wrapped in a fabric *Afikomen* bag or napkin and is hidden (the children will try to find it later). The smaller piece of the broken *matzah* is replaced with the other two whole *matztot*. Then, the *matzot* are ceremoniously uncovered for all to see. The following announcement is made aloud:

> **This is the bread of poverty which our ancestors ate in the land of Egypt. All who are hungry, come and eat. All who are needy, come and celebrate Passover with us. Now we celebrate here. Next year, may we be in the land of Israel. Now we are slaves. Next year, may we be truly free.**

The wine cups are filled a second time. No one drinks them yet.

5. *Maggid* (Questions, Story and second cup of wine)
5a. Four Questions
The leader exclaims, "**how different is this night from all others!**" By custom, this part of the *seder* involves the youngest child present asking the famous Four Questions to the leader of the *seder*. The Four Questions are the following:

> **1. On all other nights, we eat bread or *matzah*.
> On this night, why do we only eat *matzah*?**
>
> **2. On all other nights, we eat all kind of vegetables.
> On this night, why do we eat only *maror* (bitter herbs)?**
>
> **3. On all other nights, we do not have to dip our vegetables even once.
> On this night, why do we dip them twice?**
>
> **4. On all other nights, we eat our meals sitting any way we like.
> On this night, why do we lean on pillows?**

The leader begins to answer with the following:

This night is different from all other nights because once we were slaves to Pharaoh in Egypt, but Adonai, our God, took us out with His mighty hand and His outstretched arm. If Adonai had not brought our ancestors out of Egypt, then we and all of our people and descendants would still be enslaved. We know the story and tell it many times, but it is a sacred duty to hold this story of our salvation as an important part of our memory. This night is also different because, whereas once we were in idolatry, now we only worship our God, Adonai, the One Who is everywhere. Praised be our Deliverer.

Baruch Hamakom Baruch Hu.

Baruch Shenatan Torah lamo Yisrael Baruch Hu.

Praised be God Who is Everywhere. Praised be God.
Praised be God who gave the *Torah* to the people of Israel.
Praised be God.

5b. Four Children

The next section tells of the Four Children. The early authors of the *haggadah* recognized that the reactions to learning of Passover differed with each person. When teaching children, especially, a parent may be confronted with one of four major reactions. These four categories are represented by children who are, in turn, wise, wicked, simple and ignorant. The leader then discusses each one:

[Upon learning of Passover] the wise child might ask, "What is the meaning of the laws and rules with Adonai our God has commanded us?" To this child, we must explain all the laws and customs of Passover in great detail. The wicked child might ask, "What does this service mean to you?"

Since this child does not include himself in the service and denies ownership of the celebration, we answer, "we celebrate Passover because of what Adonai did for us. If you had been in Egypt with such feelings, you would not have been freed with us." The simple child might ask, "What is this all about?" We are to reply, "Adonai freed us from Egypt with a might hand." Also, a child might not know enough to ask (often called "the ignorant child"). To this child, we must explain that we do this service in a joyful and grateful remembrance of God freeing us as slaves in Egypt.

5c. Passover Story and Plagues

The Passover story is retold at this time (similar to the story that this Passover chapter begins with). Special emphasis is spent in retelling each of the plagues of Egypt. Each time a plague is mentioned, a bit of wine symbolizing "joy" is spilled out of our cup in empathy for the Egyptians, who were also God's children. This is done by dipping a spoon or finger into the cup and bringing a drop out of the cup and onto a plate or dish) to reduce the total volume of the cup with the mention of each grievous plague.[54] Each one is said slowly and solemnly.

Blood

Frogs

Lice

Beasts

Livestock diseases

Boils

Hail

---

[54] Note: You can also use symbols accompanying each plague such as little plastic frogs, locusts, livestock (with disease "spots" painted on them) and beast figures. We also use ping pong balls for hail and blackened goggles or sun glasses to represent darkness. Use your imagination!

Locusts

Darkness

Plague of the firstborn

<u>5d. God's Promise</u>
The Passover story continues with the telling of Pharaoh's determination to pursue and recapture the people of Israel. God saved Israel by defeating her enemies.

Numerous times in our history, enemies have tried to destroy us, but the Jewish people live on [according to God's promise].

Have a participant read *Psalm 114* at this time:

When Israel went down from Egypt, the house of Jacob from a people of strange language, Judah became His sanctuary, Israel His dominion. The sea looked and fled; The Jordan turned back. The mountains skipped like rams, the hills, like lambs. What ails you, O sea, that you flee? O Jordan, that you turn back? O mountains, that you skip like rams? O hills, like lambs? Tremble, O earth, before the Lord, before the God of Jacob, Who turned the rock into a pool of water, the flint into a fountain of water.[55]

<u>5e. Dayenu</u>
God has shown His people so many acts of kindness, generosity and goodness. Each one would have been enough. The leader says each line below with the other participants saying in unison "*dayenu*" which means in Hebrew, "that alone would have been enough, for that alone we are grateful."[56]

---

[55] NASB
[56] This is a popular Passover song. The tune and Hebrew lyrics can be found online by searching "*Dayenu.*"

Adonai took us out of Egypt (all reply *dayenu*)

Punished the Egyptians, destroying their gods (all reply *dayenu*)

Divided the sea and led us across on dry land (all reply *dayenu*)

Took care of us in the desert, feeding us manna (all reply *dayenu*)

Gave us *Shabbat* (all reply *dayenu*)

Brought us to Mount Sinai and gave us *Torah* (all reply *dayenu*)

Brought us to Israel and built the Holy Temple (all reply *dayenu*)

For all these, alone and together, we say (together, all say *dayenu*)

5f. Passover Symbols Explained

The three most important symbols of the Passover *seder* are explained:
   While raising the shank bone or equivalent:

> **This is called the *Pesach*, or Passover. It points to the lamb that was sacrificed by our ancestors and eaten for the Passover meal. This shank bone is a reminder of the tenth plague when, due to the sacrificed lamb (with its blood spread on the door posts) the homes of the Israelites were spared from the death of the first born.**

While raising the *matzah*:

> **We eat this *matzah* to remind us of our ancestors leaving Egypt with such haste that they did not have time to let the bread rise.**

While raising the *maror* or bitter herb:

> **We eat this *maror*, or bitter herb, lest we forget the bitterness of slavery imposed upon our people by the Egyptians. We know the sweetness of freedom best after understanding the bitterness of bondage.**

5g. Songs of Praise

All lift wine cups (without drinking) and say:

> We have a duty to give thanks, sing praises and to bless the Holy One who delivered us from Egypt through miracles, for bringing us from slavery to freedom, from sadness to joy, from darkness to light. All of us who live now are still part of the ancient struggle and are free today because of this deliverance by the Divine Hand. In every generation, we must imagine ourselves as having personally been delivered from Egypt and slavery. Therefore, we all bless Adonai for his redemption.

(All say together): **Hallelujah.**

> Give praise to Adonai. Sing praises, all we who serve Him. Blessed is His name now and forever more.

5f. The Second Cup

(Lift full cups):

> Blessed are you O Lord God, King of the Universe, who has freed our people from Egyptian slavery and brought us to this night when we eat the *matzah* and *maror*. We praise you as we celebrate the *seder*, eating the offering and symbolic sacrifices while singing praises for our redemption.
>
> *Baruch ata Adonai, Eloheinu Melech ha-olam, boray peri hagafen.* (Amen).

In English:

> **Blessed are You, Lord our God, King of the universe, Who creates the fruit of the vine. (Amen).**

Drink the cup at this time while leaning to the left side. Once the cup is empty, have the person next to you refill it.

6. _Rachtzah_ (We wash our hands for the meal and say the blessing)

   Baruch ata Adonai, Eloheinu Melech ha-olam, asher kideshanu bemitzvotav vetzivanu al netilat yada'yim. (Amen).

   In English:

   Blessed are You Lord our God, King of the universe, Who has sanctified us with His commandments and commanded us concerning the washing of hands. (Amen).

7. _Motzi/ matzah_ (We say the blessing for "bread" and _matzah_)
Distribute pieces of the upper and middle *matzah* to participants.

   Baruch ata Adonai Eloheinu Melech ha-olam, ha-motzi lechem min ha-aretz.. (Amen).

   In English:

   Blessed are You, Lord our God, King of the universe, who brings forth bread of the earth. (Amen).

   Baruch ata Adonai, Eloheinu Melech ha-olam, asher kideshanu bemitzvotav vetzivanu al achilat matzah. (Amen).

   In English:

   Blessed are You Lord our God, King of the universe, Who has sanctified us with His commandments and commanded us concerning eating the *matzah*.

   We eat the *matzah* now as the *Torah* commands us, "seven days you shall eat unleavened bread." This *matzah* also reminds us of the bread our ancestors ate while fleeing Egypt. (Amen).

   The *matzah* is now eaten together while leaning to the left side.

8. _Maror_ (We dip the _maror_ into the _charoset_ and say a blessing)
Each participant takes a small spoonful of _maror_ and _charoset_ and eats them together after the following blessing is recited:

Baruch ata Adonai, Eloheinu Melech ha-olam, asher kideshanu bemitzvotav vetzivanu al achilat maror. (Amen).

In English:

Blessed are You Lord our God, King of the universe, Who has sanctified us with His commandments and commanded us concerning eating bitter herbs. (Amen).

9. _Korech_ (We eat "Hillel's sandwich" followed by third cup)
Each participant takes a small spoonful of _maror_ and _charoset_ and eats them together with bottom _matzah_ and (bitter) lettuce, making a "Hillel Sandwich." As much _charoset_ as desired can be used here to offset the required bitter components of the sandwich.

10. _Shulchan Orech_ (Dinner)
Dinner is served.

11. _Tzafun_ (We eat the _Afikomen_ "dessert")
After the _Afikomen_ is found and ransomed, it is divided amongst everyone to eat as the dessert of the meal. It is technically part of the meal, so no blessing is needed. Nothing should be eaten after the _Afikomen_, as it should be the last thing to be savored in the mouth.

12. _Barech_ (We say the blessing after the meal, have the third cup of wine and welcome the prophet Elijah)
The third cup of wine is readied (glasses are filled now if not already full). A blessing after the meal is said followed by a blessing over the wine:

Blessed are you, Lord God, king of the universe who gives food to the world with goodness, mercy and kindness. Your

love endures forever, so we praise you, the Provider of all life. May You, Who makes peace in Heaven, make peace for us, for Israel, and the whole world.

12a. Third cup
All raise full cups together:

Baruch ata Adonai, Eloheinu Melech ha-olam, boray peri hagafen.

In English:

Blessed are You, Lord our God, King of the universe, Who creates the fruit of the vine.

All drink the cups. The person sitting next to you is to refill them again.

12b. Welcoming Elijah
The front door is opened (usually by a child) for the greeting of Elijah, as he is to preceded the Messiah's coming. (Christians believe that this Elijah figure was fulfilled with the coming of John the Baptist).

May Elijah the Prophet come soon to us in our day, heralding in the time of the Messiah.

13. *Hallel* (Songs of praise)
Assorted praise songs are sung at this time.

14. *Nirtzah* (We complete the *seder*)
Fourth cup
All raise full cups together:

Baruch ata Adonai, Eloheinu Melech ha-olam, boray peri hagafen. (Amen).

In English:

Blessed are You, Lord our God, King of the universe, Who creates the fruit of the vine. (Amen).

All drink.
Leader concludes:

Appropriately, our *haggadah* ends on a triumphant note of victory and praise. May the sincerity and passion that we have brought to our celebration of the Passover be present in our lives throughout the year. Truth, justice, mercy and kindness are the opposite of slavery, persecution and oppression. May we embody these traits and be granted the blessing of celebrating the Passover for many years to come.

All say in unison:

Next year in Jerusalem!

FEAST OF UNLEAVENED BREAD (MATZOT)

On the Jewish calendar: 15-21(22) *Nissan* (March-April)

...Celebrate the Feast of Unleavened Bread... eat bread made without yeast, as I commanded you. Do this at the appointed time in the month of Abib [Aviv] for in that month you came out of Egypt. No one is to appear before me empty-handed.[57]

HOLIDAY BACKGROUND

During the days of Passover, unleavened bread, or *matzah*, is eaten in honor of this holiday. The absence of leaven during the holiday is in observance of this feast. This is to remind those who observe the day of the flight from Egypt. The particular haste of the escape was apparent by the way that the bread had no time to rise.

In scripture, leaven has taken on other meanings such as wickedness and sin. The holiday Unleavened Bread assumes both these connotations.

---

[57] Exodus 23:14-15

TRADITIONAL OBSERVANCE

Before this holiday period[58] can be fully celebrated, much preparation must go into readying the household. First, all *chametz* (leaven) must be removed from the dwelling to be either destroyed (usually burned) or sold. The dried *arba minim* (the four agricultural species used during Sukkot—see *Sukkot* section) may be burned at this time in accordance to some of the traditions.[59] The *chametz* itself includes all products made of fermented wheat, rye, barley, oats or malt. Sometimes corn, rice and legumes are also included in this prohibition since they can be ground and made into flour/bread. The purpose for this is obedience to the mandate of God: "For seven days you are to eat bread made without yeast. On the first day *remove the yeast from your houses,* for whoever eats anything with yeast in it from the first day through the seventh must be cut off from Israel."[60] The abstention from leaven includes regular and otherwise unleavened flour and grain products that may have been subject to natural leavening. When moisture comes into contact with flour or grain for over eighteen minutes, leaven becomes naturally produced, say rabbis. Thus, unless the collection, milling processes, and subsequent baking have been closely watched by rabbis to ensure that this has not happened, the food item is not considered free from leaven or kosher for Passover. This is why some otherwise "unleavened" breads and even *matzot* are not "kosher" for Passover.

JESUS IN THE PASSOVER (YESHUA IN PESACH)

The Passover is the prime foreshadowing of the coming of the Messiah and redemption in him. On this very day, the Passover lamb was sacrificed.

---

[58] Judaism recognizes the Passover to include both the actual Passover (one day) and the Feast of Unleavened Bread (one week), thus yielding a total of *eight days* of Passover as traditionally observed.
[59] Some Orthodox Jews such as those of *Chabad Lubavitch* adhere to this tradition.
[60] Exodus 12:15

On this very day, Yeshua also had to be killed—or else he would not be our Passover Lamb at all! The Passover is emphasized heavily in the *Torah* for good reason; this holiday of the literal blood of the Passover lamb is the main pointer to humanity's coming salvation through the blood of the divine Passover Lamb, in the figurative sense. Passover is crucial in pointing to our ultimate salvation. The holiday is of supreme importance. *Nissan* is often considered the "first month" so that this holiday is the focal point by which the others are referenced.[61]

> Though other cycles and other aspects of life in the LORD are important, it is the sacrifice of the Lamb that gives it all meaning. Except for the sacrifice of the Passover and the blood on the door posts, Israel would have suffered the same fate as the Egyptians. The promises to Abraham, Isaac, and Jacob would have then become void.... Apart from the sacrifice of the Passover and the blood on the doorposts, there would have been no basis for Messiah, our Passover, to be sacrificed on the anniversary of that momentous occasion. We would have no hope and remained dead in our sins (Sampson, 111).

This holiday's month can be appropriately considered "first." The first month of the year is the beginning of life, not just life as in "seasonal" life, but in spiritual life—life everlasting.

YESHUA'S FULFILLMENT

The following correlations below, borrowed in part from Elwood McQuaid, illustrate our Savior's role as fulfillment and completion of the Passover holiday:

---

[61] Although *Nissan* is considered to be the "first" month in Judaism, *Tishrei* (the beginnig of the agricultural year) was also used to calculate Sabbath and Jubilee years (*The Mishnah*, 299). *Tishrei* can also be considered to be the "fiscal" year of annul repentance.

Deliverance from judgment through the lamb. This was the means of salvation. The blood of the slain lamb proved to be protection for the first born of manner the physical and literal lamb and its blood saved the inhabitants of the house, so does the blood of our Heavenly Lamb save us from certain death

Deliverance from the enemy. This step also sanctified the nation of Israel and made them a people "set apart" for God and his purposes. This part of the observance named them as God's chosen people. By accepting the blood of the divine Lamb, all believers become part of the body of the Messiah. Grafted into [which doesn't mean "replacing"] the divinely chosen nation, they also become sanctified and "set apart."

Deliverance to enter the land. *When you enter the land that the LORD will give you as He promised, observe this ceremony (Exodus 12:25).* This also set in motion the beginning of the fulfillment of the assurance of inheriting the "Promised Land." The divine plan was to climax in granting these Chosen People their Promised Land. Likewise, the Christian, as grafted into the nation of Chosen People is promised a heavenly land ruled by their Messianic King.

New beginning. *This month is to be for you the first month, the first month of your year (Exodus 12:2).* This was the start of a new age. Just as the ancient Jewish nation entered a new beginning, so the Christian does also upon living for and with the Savior.

Lamb selected. *Tell the whole community of Israel that on the tenth day of this month each man is to take a lamb for his family, one for each household (Exodus 12:3).* The lamb had to be chosen by each house during this time. Likewise, the Christian today must exercise his/her power of choice in choosing his/her God. Will he/she choose the Lamb of God. Will He be King of their lives?

Lamb scrutinized. *The animals you choose must be year-old males without defect, and you may take them from the sheep or the goats. Take care of them until the fourteenth day of the month, when all the people of the community of Israel must slaughter them at twilight (Exodus 12:5-6).* The lamb was to be without blemishes or spots. Pure and perfect was this Passover lamb. The Savior who came not only to just the Jewish people but to all of humanity, was to be perfect and without guile or sin. Just as the shepherds had to ensure that the lambs they raised for the sacrifice were identified as pure, so the shepherds attended the birth of the Savior, ensuring the worthiness of the Lamb.

Lamb slain. *Take care of them until the fourteenth day of the month, when all the people of the community of Israel must slaughter them at twilight. Then they are to take some of the blood and put it on the sides and tops of the doorframes of the houses where they eat the lambs (Exodus 12:6-7).* The only way for the saving blood to be spilled was for the lamb to be slain. This was the only acceptable solution. Like this literal lamb, so the Lamb of God had to be slain for the shedding of the redemptive blood.

Lamb sufficient. *If any household is too small for a whole lamb, they must share one with their nearest neighbor, having taken into account the number of people there are. You are to determine the amount of lamb needed in accordance with what each person will eat.... That same night they are to eat the meat roasted over the fire, along with bitter herbs, and bread made without yeast. (Exodus 12:4,8).* The amount needed for each person was to be determined. Each person was to have his/her share. No one was to go without some of the Passover lamb, as today no one is to go without the saving blood of the Lamb. The lamb had to be sufficient for the entire household, as the Heavenly Lamb is. They were to feast on it in fellowship together. The unleavened bread was to be eaten in symbolism of the haste of leaving Egypt without time for it to rise. The bitter herbs served as reminders of the harsh bondage and suffering.

Lamb saving. *The blood will be a sign for you on the houses where you are; and when I see the blood, I will pass over you. No destructive plague will touch you when I strike Egypt (Exodus 12:13).* The blood as a sign on the houses saved the occupants from death. So, just as this Passover lamb's blood saved the lives of others by its own death and blood, our divine Lamb saves us from the wages of our sin—eternal death.

Lamb sustaining. *This is a day you are to commemorate; for the generations to come (Exodus 12:14a).* [Notice it says "for the generations to come." This implies forever and not just until the fulfillment of the cross]. The sustenance of the nation was directly correlated with their keeping of the festival and commemoration of the Passover. The spiritual sustenance of the Messianic believer is the same today—totally dependent upon our faith and taking hold of the salvation provided us.

Lamb suggesting. *…You shall celebrate it as a festival to the LORD—a lasting ordinance (Exodus 12:14b).* The "lasting ordinance" here implies a future importance. The prophetic undertones are pointing to a future event by which this is symbolized. "One day the Lamb will replace lambs" (McQuaid 40-42).

The power of the symbolism is wholly apparent when analyzed this way. There is a direct correlation between the actual and the symbol, between what was then and what was to come. Yeshua was always at the heart of this Passover feast. He was and is still central to all that it stands for.

AFIKOMEN

Interesting to note is the significance of the traditional "hunt for the *Afikomen*" that most Jewish households are familiar with. This is a time during the feast of unleavened bread when a piece of *matzah* is wrapped in a cloth and hidden. Often, a surprise or gift is offered to the child who finds it. This itself is deeply symbolic. Just as the body of Yeshua was broken, wrapped in grave clothes and hidden in a tomb, only to be revealed and risen anew, so this piece of *matzah* is broken, wrapped in cloth or a napkin and hidden out of sight to be found, revealed, displayed and eaten as the honored and special "dessert." Fischer explains,

> Now as we celebrate *Pesach*, we remember not only God's actions during the time of the Exodus but also Yeshua's death for us, which secured our atonement. In fact, the term used for the piece of *matzah* which is "hidden" during the *Pesach* meal, *Afikomen*—a Greek, not Hebrew term— literally means "the one who came" (Fischer, 2004: accessed 04 Aug 2010).

Most mainstream Jews, who do not even believe that Yeshua is the Messiah, faithfully observe this tradition annually.

HOW CAN THIS BENEFIT YOU, A CHRISTIAN?

While Christians revere the Eucharist and approach the Lord's Supper with solemnity, it must be remembered that Passover is Jewish holiday of celebrating victory and life. Passover is about being free and liberated to serve our God. While images of the sacrificial Lamb does invoke sadness, the day itself is dedicated to the celebration of the triumph and victory of God for His people. Therefore, the day should be celebrated with gaiety and joy.

For a Christian today, there is still so much spiritual richness that can be taken and embraced from the Passover feast. Even aside from the fact that the Savior is central to this feast, this holiday week has much for all believers to benefit from. Christians ought to take this holiday and embrace it for what it stands for—a beautiful symbolic portrait of our Savior's life and triumph (although dearly bought) for us. The whole holiday points to the liberation of God's people and our Yeshua, the means by which we are free and live. Surely a sincere follower would therefore be interested.

Furthermore, who has not been delivered from a spiritual Egypt at some time—poverty, unemployment, failure, discouragement, depression, destructive relationships, disease or sickness? This is a time of rejoicing and reflecting upon the deliverance that we have experienced through God in our own lives. All of us at some stage in life have needed deliverance or freedom, rescue or aid. God works in our lives constantly. Contemplate and reflect what this means to you in your individual life's circumstances.

HOLIDAY NOSHES (SNACKS)

This is one of my family's favorites. My children beg for this all year long! It is easy as well as truly tasty. It closely resembles regular lasagna in flavor and texture, yet it is delightfully kosher for Passover.

MATZAH LASAGNA (dairy)

Ingredients

- 1 16 oz bottle of Spaghetti sauce or marinara
- 1/2 pint cottage cheese
- 1/8 teaspoon oregano
- 1 cup canned corn
- 1/2 cup black (mild) olives
- 6 whole *matzah* crackers dampened with warm water
- 2 cups mozzarella cheese, grated
- 1/2 cup Parmesan cheese, grated

Variation

- 1/2 cup canned mushrooms may be added
- 1 cup vegetarian meat substitute may be added
- Stir ingredients together for more texture instead of blending (see next)

Directions

1. Put marinara sauce, corn, olives, cottage cheese, oregano (and mushrooms if desired) into a blender.
2. Blend until smooth.
3. Combine mozzarella and Parmesan cheeses together.
4. Line 9 x 13 casserole dish with sauce 1/4 inch deep. Spread evenly.
5. Cover with single-layer *matzah* crackers broken into strips, as you would use lasagna noodles.
6. Spread sauce on this layer 1/4 inch deep.
7. Sprinkle a layer of mozzarella and parmesan cheeses (and vegetarian meat if desired).
8. Add another layer of *matzah* crackers.
9. Spread with sauce as before and then cheese.
10. Repeat until dish is full.
11. Bake at 350 for 45 minutes.
12. Serve hot.
13. ENJOY!

Once again, here is a holiday favorite in our home. It has earned many compliments at Passover *seder* dinner.

CHAROSET (pareve)

Ingredients

- 6 tart apples—peeled, cored, grated
- 3 teaspoons honey
- 1/2 cup raisins
- 1/2 cup grape juice (use this for soaking the raisins)
- 1 teaspoon ground cinnamon

- 1/8 teaspoon ground allspice
- 1/2-3/4 cup chopped nuts (walnuts, almonds or pecans)
- 1/2 cup raisins (soaked in the 1/2 cup grape juice / wine)

Variation

- 1/4 cup pomegranate juice can be used for the grape juice for the raisin soak
- 1/2 cup dried cranberries can be substituted for raisins
- 1/4 cup finely chopped apricots add more color

Directions

1. Soak raisins until puffy. Heating the raisins and juice in the microwave or stovetop may accelerate this process.
2. Mix grated apples, honey, juice, raisins, cinnamon, allspice and nuts together.
3. Refrigerate until use.
4. Stir before serving. The type of apples used will dictate the moisture of the mix. If it is too wet, drain off some of the excess liquid. If too dry, add a bit more fruit juice.
5. Serve cold.
6. Enjoy!

FEAST OF FIRST FRUITS (BIKKURIM)

On Jewish calendar: 16 *Nissan* (March-April)

Then the LORD spoke to Moses, saying, "Speak to the sons of Israel and say to them, 'When you enter the land which I am going to give to you and reap its harvest, then you shall bring in the sheaf of the first fruits of your harvest to the priest. He shall wave the sheaf before the LORD for you to be accepted; on the day after the Sabbath the priest shall wave it. Now on the day when you wave the sheaf, you shall offer a male lamb one year old without defect for a burn offering to the LORD. Its grain offering shall then be two-tenths of an ephah of fine flour mixed with oil, and offering by fire to the LORD for a soothing aroma, with its drink offering, a fourth of a hin of wine. Until this same day, until you have brought in the offering of your God, you shall eat neither bread nor roasted grain nor new growth. It is to be a perpetual statute throughout your generations in all your dwelling places.'"[62]

---

[62] Leviticus 23:9-14 NASB

HOLIDAY BACKGROUND

This is part of the Passover celebration that officially has its own significance. This is considered the early "first fruits" of harvest time, with *Shavuot* being the later one (see next holiday).

This was also the beginning of the barley harvest. The Israelites would bring a sheaf, or wave offering, to the Temple. This day would mark the beginning of the official Counting of the Omer (barley sheaves):

> *From the day after the Sabbath, the day you brought the sheaf of the wave offering, count off seven full weeks. Count off fifty days up to the day after the seventh Sabbath, and then present an offering of new grain to the LORD.*[63]

This count is often kept with a blessing said for each day of the Omer in a count from Passover to the Feast of Weeks. It denotes a promise of that greater part of the harvest which is to come. It has also been a day of miracles outdone only by Passover. It never became one of the High Holy Days, nor is it a "Sabbath" rest day; however it is still a special day.

The *Omer* count is a somewhat solemn time in modern traditional Judaism. Rabbinical accounts speak of a terrible plague that killed many but began to wane on the 33rd day of the *Omer*. Since that time, this thirty-third day of the *Omer* (or *Lag B'Omer*) is a holiday celebrated by traditional Jews. On this day, Israel celebrates with picnics, archery, weddings, and oddly enough, haircuts—especially "first" haircuts for two-year old boys. This is not a biblical holiday, but may be celebrated for the sake of solidarity with the Jewish people.

WHAT DOES THIS MEAN FOR YOU, A CHRISTIAN?

On the day of First Fruits, Yeshua conquered death. Despite not being "discovered" by humanity until the morning, his rising from the dead

---

[63] Leviticus 23:15-16

itself was likely to have happened shortly after the closing of the Sabbath, as sunset heralds the beginning of the new day in Jewish tradition. Christians celebrate Easter as the day of the risen Lord, however, according to the Jewish calendar, we can see that it was on First Fruits that he rose. Scripture points this out:

> ***But now Christ has been raised from the dead, the first fruits of those who are asleep. For since by a man came death, by a man also came the resurrection of the dead. For as in Adam all die, so also in Christ all will be made alive. But each in his own order: Christ the first fruits, after that those who are Christ's at His coming....*[64]**

This is significant, as it points to our Savior as being one of the "first fruits" of the resurrected dead. If we are serious about celebrating the day that the Savior rose from the dead, then First Fruits is the day of commemoration!

HOLIDAY NOSHES (SNACKS)

The Passover week is a perfect time to try out *matzah* recipes, although we often carry the *matzah* tradition on all year. This recipe of *matzah* with eggs makes a nice breakfast food. The *matzah* adds some body to the eggs and creates a nice start to the day. Eggs are always a symbol of new beginnings, so all the more, this recipe is appropriate.

MATZAH BREI (pareve)

Ingredients

- 3 *matzah* crackers
- 3 eggs

---

[64] I Corinthians 15:20-23 NASB

- 1/8 teaspoon salt or to taste
- Oil for frying

Variation

- Add 1/2 teaspoon cinnamon and 1 tablespoon honey for sweet flavor
- Add 1/3 chopped onion and 1/2 teaspoon dill for savory flavor

Directions

1. Crumble the *matzah crackers* and soak them in warm water for 3 minutes.
2. Lightly beat eggs
3. Add salt (and/or sweet flavorings) to egg mixture
4. Drain *matzah pieces*
5. Mix *matzah* pieces and eggs together
6. Drop approximately 1/3 cup of mixture onto hot fry pan
7. Turn over and fry until golden brown
8. ENJOY!

ISRAELI MEMORIAL DAY (YOM HAZIKARON)

On the Jewish calendar: 4th of *Iyyar* (Apr-May)

A civic holiday, rather than religious, is the Memorial Day of Israel. The Israeli Knesset (Parliament) declared this day to be a memorial time set aside for the remembrance of all those who lost their lives in the struggle for Israel's independence as well as all those who have been killed while on active duty in the Israeli forces. Due to the Arab intifada and the increased terrorist activity in Israel, many Jews also add to their memorial and remembrance the security forces who have given their lives in trying to protect Israeli citizens from terrorist attacks. For many, this expanded list of "the remembered" also includes the victims of terrorism.

Memorializing and remembering those of us who have gone before is a very prominent feature in Jewish culture. As on *Yom Hashoah*, the lives of those who have passed on are remembered with respect on *Yom HaZikaron*. Like those in the Holocaust, the soldiers who gave their lives for their State of Israel died untimely deaths. The difference is that they died fighting, buying with their very blood the independence that Israel enjoys today.

TRADITIONAL OBSERVANCE

The mood of this Israeli Memorial Day is not exactly like the American Memorial Day. Although the days in both countries are used to commemorate the military heroes lost, in Israel, an extra measure of sobriety is added. On this day, all pubs, theaters, cinemas, nightclubs and other places of public entertainment are closed. The country stops all traffic and daily activities and observes two periods of silence preceded by a loud siren. Drivers stop their cars and stand outside their vehicles as a sign of respect. This occurs at 8 o'clock in the evening at the onset of the day (remember, sunset of the previous night ushers in the Jewish holidays) and then sounds again at 11 o'clock in the late morning before the prayers are read at the military cemeteries. The radio broadcasts songs and poems related to the remembrance theme, and stories of the heroes lost are retold on the airwaves.

Official religious tradition has not yet taken hold on this holiday, as it is still mostly a civic occasion; however, the awe and sanctity of the day (enough to rival any religious ceremony) seems quite apparent, especially during the observance surrounding the eerie sounding of the siren. Some synagogues observe *Yom Ha'Atzmaut* by adding a special reading to the service which often precedes the mourner's prayer (*kaddish*). Israel's Independence day, although a time of rejoicing and celebration is made all the more meaningful and appreciated due to its proximity to *Yom HaZikaron*, this day set aside to remember all those who died for the cause of an independent Israel.

As the day fades into the sunset of a the next day, a ceremony is often held to both close the Israeli Memorial Day and to usher in Israel's Independence Day. Mount Herzl, Jerusalem often is the site of such celebration featuring military parades displaying Israel's flag, a ceremonial lighting of twelve beacons to represent the twelve tribes of Israel, and speeches by members of the *Knesset* (Israeli Parliament).

ISRAEL'S INDEPENDENCE DAY
(YOM HA'ATZMAUT)

On the Jewish calendar: 5th of *Iyyar* (Apr-May)

This is a very young and modern holiday, relatively speaking. This day is also known as Israel's Independence Day. Like July fourth to the United States, this day is met with much patriotism and joyous celebration of the Israeli national identity. After centuries (almost two millennia) of persecution, exile and rejection from other nations, the Jewish people were finally granted their own land again. In this land, Israel triumphantly declared her own independence in 1948.

Upon this momentous occasion, Ben Gurion[65] declared *Yom Ha'Atzmaut*, the official day of Israel's independence, with these words:

> The Land of Israel was the birthplace of the Jewish people. Here the spiritual, religious and national identity was formed. Here they achieved independence and created a culture of national and universal significance. Here they wrote and gave the Bible to the world.... Exiled from Palestine, the Jewish people remained faithful to it in all the countries of the

---

[65] Ben Gurion (1886-1973) was the first Prime Minister of Israel and one of the founders of the State of Israel.

dispersion, never ceasing to pray and hope for their return and restoration of their national freedom. Accordingly, we, the members of the National Council met together in solemn assembly today and by virtue of the national and historic right of the Jewish people and with the support of the resolution of the General of the United Nations, hereby proclaim the establishment of the Jewish state in Palestine to be called Israel.... We offer peace and amity to all neighboring states and their peoples and invite them to cooperate with the independent Jewish nation for the common good of all... With trust in the Rock of Israel, we set our hands to this declaration at this session of the Provisional State Council in the city of Tel Aviv on Sabbath Eve, 5th Iyyar 5708, 14th day of May 1948 (Jewish Virtual Library).

The announcement was broadcast to a vast world audience. Within twenty-four hours, several neighboring Arab countries banded together, declaring war on the infant State. Many feared for Israel, as the Arabs threatened less of a war and more of a slaughter, another holocaust of sorts due to the odds (one hundred to one). Nevertheless, Israel was not so easily vanquished. Their stake to their land was upheld—they survived a battle that proved to be nothing short of a *miracle* in their favor. Notwithstanding, the battle was still a bloody one. Many of Israel's sons died as soldiers in that fight. Thus, a memorial day for fallen soldiers (*Yom Hazikaron*) immediately precedes *Yom Ha'atzmaut*. Memorial Day gives way to Independence Day as the sun slips beneath the horizon. The significance of the proximity of these two important days is simply thus: if not for the sacrifice of the fallen soldiers, an independent Israel would not exist. The nation of Israel mourns and remembers the fallen and then celebrates that costly freedom that the blood of those precious lost has bought.

Yom Ha'atzmaut is additionally important to many religious Jews due to the prophecy that such a unification and re-establishment of the nation of Israel would precede ultimate redemption—the coming of the long awaited messiah.

MODERN ISRAEL IN PROPHECY

Moses predicted both the exile of the Jewish people from "the land" as well as their return (Deuteronomy 30:4-5). The Jewish people have been scattered around the globe for almost two thousand years and yet are gathered again as one nation and one people with their Hebrew tongue being spoken once more as not just a religious dialect, but as an everyday language. This alone puts modern Israel into the context of prophecy for many. Thousands of nations and peoples have come and then disappeared since ancient times, yet few remain—and none who have been so actively persecuted as the Jewish people. For thousands of years, other nations and national leaders have sought to minimize Jewish numbers or to eradicate them altogether. Typified in scripture as the Egyptian Pharaoh and Haman of Persia and also by those such as Hitler and Hamas in more recent times, the enemies of the Jews have sought diligently and systematically to erase the Jewish nation. The sheer fact that the Jewish people remain through all this over time is a testament to their divine promise and the prophecy surrounding the Jewish people.

TRADITIONAL OBSERVANCE

As mentioned above, *Yom Ha'Atzmaut* is greeted at the dawn of *Yom HaZikaron*. One holiday merges into the other with a corresponding significance that lends itself to a deeper appreciation of the overall theme of Israeli nationalism. On this day, Israelis are not alone in celebration. Jews the world over observe the day in showing solidarity with Israel. In Israel, if the holiday falls on a Friday or *Shabbat*, it is celebrated the previous Thursday. Like the Americans during the Fourth of July, Israelis celebrate with parades, parties, fireworks and the singing of their national anthem (*HaTikvah*). As previously mentioned, the day is greeted with ceremonies to include the festivities and speeches on Mount Herzl, Jerusalem, as *Yom HaZikaron* fades.

For Jews outside of Israel, it is commonly celebrated on the closest Sunday with many Israeli-themed festivities and dishes. Often a quiz with questions centered on Israel is featured so as to increase the awareness of Israel and the many benefits it has contributed to the modern world. The celebrated independent and unique identity of Israel helps to answer the question posed by Israelis, as "who are we?"

Religious traditions are slower in developing. The actual spiritual character of the day is still under scrutiny and debate, as differing Jewish circles have yet to come to a common religious assessment of the day. As time progresses, certainly more tradition will develop around the day. For now, the Chief Rabbinate of the State of Israel has prescribed the singing of Psalms and a reading of a prophetic portion of scripture. Many Jewish congregations include such special readings and a singing of the *HaTikvah* while most of the Ultra-Orthodox, who believe the State of Israel is nothing more than a synthetic invention created by human hands, do not agree with this observance.

FEAST OF WEEKS AND PENTECOST (SHAVUOT)

On the Jewish calendar: 6 *Sivan* (May-June)

From the day after the Sabbath, the day you brought the sheaf of the wave offering, count off seven full weeks. Count off fifty days up to the day after the seventh Sabbath, and then present an offering of new grain to the LORD. From wherever you live, bring two loaves made of two-tenths of an ephah of fine flour, baked with yeast, as a wave offering of first fruits to the LORD. Present with this bread seven male lambs, each a year old and without defect, one young bull and two rams. They will be a burnt offering to the LORD, together with their grain offerings and drink offerings—an offering made by fire, an aroma pleasing to the LORD. Then sacrifice one male goat for a sin offering and two lambs, each a year old, for a fellowship offering. The priest is to wave the two lambs before the LORD as a wave offering, together with the bread of the first fruits. They are a sacred offering to the LORD for the priest. On that same day you are to proclaim a sacred assembly and do no regular work. This is to be a lasting ordinance for the generations to come, wherever you live.[66]

---

[66] Leviticus 23:15-21

HOLIDAY BACKGROUND

After the Jewish nation had their first official Passover and crossed through the Red Sea,[67] they found themselves camped at the base of Mount Sinai. During this time, they rejoiced over their triumphant escape from the Egyptians. They were led in songs by Miriam the cantor, or song leader. Aaron also was leading the people during this time. He is noted for facilitating the creation of the golden calf and allowing the people to fall into idolatry during this time. Soon after this incident, Moses came down from Mount Sinai with the tablets of stone with the Ten Commandments written upon them by the finger of God, only to dash them to pieces upon spying the Israelite camp reveling and making themselves merry around the golden calf. He had to go up to the mountain again to have a new set of commandments in stone. The time period between Passover and the receiving of the commandments (and oral law) was forty-nine days, or the duration of the Omer count. The end of these forty-nine days marked a special day that became known as *Shavuot*, or as some call it, the Feast of Weeks. (Later to be known as *Pentecost* by Christians).

Much more than simply a "giving of the law," this time is important, as it marks the anniversary of the covenant between God and the nation of Israel. At Sinai, a marriage-type of agreement, such as a marriage, took place. With the sign of the covenant being the observance of the seventh-day Sabbath (the fourth commandment), the *ketubah* (wedding vows)-type agreement was set into place. Although Israel had already been designated as God's people, it was at Sinai that God pledged His love for them by giving them a *Torah* for them to follow as their pledge of love back to Him. They agreed to God's terms, "When Moses went and told the people all the LORD's words and laws, they responded with one voice, 'Everything the LORD has said we will do.'"[68] Thus the covenant was complete. Both "sides" (God and the people) said their vows and sealed this *everlasting* covenant.

---

[67] Some sources refer to it as the "Reed Sea."
[68] Exodus 24:3

This was part of sanctification and being set apart. All Jews, past and present, are said to have been present at Sinai—as this was an experience that touched the very quintessence of the Jewish soul for all time. All the more, the covenant cannot ever be considered outdated or "expired," as it includes those yet unborn.

TRADITIONAL OBSERVANCE

In like manner of the holidays we have discussed previously, the ushering in of the day comes the evening. The day is opened with candles and a charitable mind, as charitable giving and hospitality is always at the fore in celebrating holidays.

CANDLES

Using the candles once again, the following blessing is recited:
The blessing is as follows:

> *Baruch ata Adonai, Eloheinu Melech ha-olam, asher kideshanu bemitzvotav vetzivanu lehadlik ner shel Yom Tov. (Amen).*

In English:

> **Blessed are You Lord our God, King of the universe, Who has sanctified us with His commandments and commanded us to kindle the festival lights. (Amen).**

Following this blessing, we add the *Shehecheyanu* as demonstrated previously:

> *Baruch ata Adonai, Eloheinu Melech ha-olam, sehecheyanu vekiyenamu, vehigianu la'zeman hazeh. (Amen).*

In English:

Blessed are You Lord our God, King of the universe, Who gave us life, and sustains us, and enabled us to reach this season of joy. (Amen).

NIGHT VIGIL WITH THE FIVE BOOKS OF MOSES (TORAH)

The Feast of Weeks (also Feast of Pentecost) is one of the main pilgrim festivals along with Passover and the Feast of Tabernacles (or Feast of Booths) that required a trip to Jerusalem for proper observance. This is a special time of thanksgiving, celebrated in both homes and synagogues. In appreciation of this "wedding" or, "anniversary" between God and the nation of Israel, it is customary to delve into the *Torah* during the holiday, staying up all night to read it together. This is one of the main ways of celebrating the day—maintaining a nocturnal vigil, immersing the mind in this *ketubah*, or marriage contract, between God and the nation of Israel.

FLOWERS

Although Mount Sinai is situated in the desert, to honor the giving of the *Torah*, the desert is said to have bloomed, sprouting flowers. In honor of this, it is traditional to decorate the house with flowers. *Shavuot* was also a day for judging fruit trees as to their prospective "fruit forecast" for the year.

PENTECOST

It was during this time that what Christians know as Pentecost took place. Have you ever read the second chapter of *Acts* and wondered why all the Jews from different places came together on this day? Realizing that it was a *Shavuot* pilgrimage makes the mystery unravel. The story of Pentecost, according to scripture is as follows:

> *When the day of Pentecost came, they were all together in one place. Suddenly a sound like the blowing of a violent wind came from heaven and filled the whole house where they were sitting. They saw what seemed to be tongues of fire that separated and came to rest on each of them. All of them were filled with the Holy Spirit and began to speak in other tongues as the Spirit enabled them. Now there were staying in Jerusalem God-fearing Jews from every nation under heaven. When they heard this sound, a crowd came together in bewilderment, because each one heard them speaking in his own language. Utterly amazed, they asked: "Are not all these men who are speaking Galileans? Then how is it that each of us hears them in his own native language? Parthians, Medes and Elamites; residents of Mesopotamia, Judea and Cappadocia, Pontus and Asia, Phrygia and Pamphylia, Egypt and the parts of Libya near Cyrene; visitors from Rome (both Jews and converts to Judaism); Cretans and Arabs-we hear them declaring the wonders of God in our own tongues!" Amazed and perplexed, they asked one another, "What does this mean?"*[69]

Notice all the different languages of the people in the room? These were not all locals, but were *Shavuot* pilgrims. The disciples and Apostles present at this famous event of Pentecost were therefore celebrating the Jewish holiday of *Shavuot*. This was after the death of the Messiah, so they obviously still observed these feasts as Sabbaths unto the Lord. Notice that they did not consider these holidays as obsolete after Yeshua's life and death on earth.

---

[69] Acts 2:1-12

JESUS IN THE FEAST OF WEEKS (or FEAST OF PENTECOST) (YESHUA IN SHAVUOT)

Soon after his resurrection, Yeshua had given the disciples specific instructions to watch for the *Ruach HaKodesh* (Holy Spirit). Scripture reads,

> *After his suffering, he showed himself to these men and gave many convincing proofs that he was alive. He appeared to them over a period of forty days and spoke about the kingdom of God. On one occasion, while he was eating with them, he gave them this command: "Do not leave Jerusalem, but wait for the gift my Father promised, which you have heard me speak about. For John baptized with water, but in a few days you will be baptized with the Holy Spirit."*[70]

Thus, on *Shavuot*, after the ascension of Yeshua, the disciples were gathered together. The Holy Spirit visited them, granting them all a portion of Himself by the physical manifestation of fire. Just as on this day, God's spirit came upon Mount Sinai, manifesting Himself through fire as the law was delivered to the world through His servant, so on this day, God's spirit came upon those in the upper room as described in *Acts*, manifesting Himself through fire as the Holy Spirit was delivered to the world through His servants. The parallel is not coincidental.

This momentous day in *Acts* became known throughout Christianity as "Pentecost." This day is also, and originally, *Shavuot*. In honoring the "Older Testament" feast of *Shavuot*, God Himself sent the Holy Spirit to humankind. Not only did the early disciples and believers in Yeshua observe and honor this festival of *Shavuot* (beyond the life and death of Yeshua on earth), but God (as Holy Spirit) did too!

---

[70] Acts 1:4-5

HOW CAN THIS BENEFIT YOU, A CHRISTIAN?

Just as the Early Church met together to observe *Shavuot*, the Christian today may take part in this blessing. God honored the early believers by pouring out His Spirit upon them. This is a special day for two reasons: 1., it is this day of Pentecost—this day that goes down in history as the outpouring of the Holy Spirit, and 2., it is the anniversary of the marriage covenant between God and the nation of Israel into which the Christian church is grafted.[71] Staying up and studying God's word on this day according to the tradition may bring unexpected joys, for we know that the words of the Lord, when read, will not be without blessing.

In the chart below, notice the parallels and similarities between the giving of the Commandments and of Pentecost, both happening on this same special day.

Shavuot / Feast of Weeks	Pentecost
The Commandments Given	The Holy Spirit Given
50 Days From the Crossing of the Red Sea	50 Days from the Resurrection of Yeshua
Law of God Written in Stone	Law of God Written on our Hearts
Three Thousand Slain	Three Thousand Receive Salvation
The Letter of the Law emphasis	The Spirit of the Law emphasis

HOLIDAY NOSHES (SNACKS)

Traditionally, *Shavuot* is a day celebrated with dairy-based foods. Since the law had just been received, the first *Shavuot* would have been met with a nation unsure with how to prepare kosher meat, as the ruling concerning *kashrut* was so new. Ice cream and custards are the children's

---

[71] Romans 11:17

favorite for the day (not to mention it is also the delight of adults, too)! Here is a traditional Jewish dairy recipe:

POTATO KUGEL (dairy)

Ingredients

- 4 cups cubed potatoes, peeled (or 4 medium potatoes)
- 3 eggs
- 1/2 cup cheddar, jack cheese (or favorite equivalent), grated
- 1/2 cup sour cream
- 1 large onion, chopped
- 1 red bell pepper, chopped
- 1 teaspoon salt
- 1 teaspoon dried sweet basil or dill
- 6 sprigs chopped parsley

Variation

- 1/2 cup carrots, grated
- 1/4 cup green onions or chives, chopped

Directions

1. Preheat oven to 350 F
2. Grease 9 x 13 casserole
3. Chop potatoes into small half-inch cubes
4. Mix remaining ingredients well.
5. Combine batter thoroughly with drained potatoes and turn into prepared casserole dish.
6. Bake 1 hour until brown.
7. Let sit for 25 minutes
8. Serve hot
9. ENJOY!

SHAVUOT CHEESE BLINTZES (dairy)

Ingredients

- 4 cups all purpose flour
- 1 1/2 cups milk
- 3 eggs
- 1/2 cup cottage cheese
- 1/2 cup sour cream
- 1 teaspoon sugar
- 1 cup fruit compote or pie filling
- Whipped cream for topping
- Oil for frying

Variation

- Ricotta may be substituted for the cottage cheese for smoother consistency
- Yogurt may be substituted for sour cream for a lower-fat option
- 1 teaspoon vanilla may be added to the filling
- Sift powdered sugar over blintz before serving

Directions

1. Heat oil in frying pan
2. Lightly beat eggs
3. Add milk to eggs, mix into batter
4. Pour 1/2 cup batter into frying pan
5. Rotate pan around to ensure an even, thin layer of batter
6. Turn over carefully with spatula after surface seems "dry"
7. Once golden, remove and drain on paper towels

8. Repeat with remaining batter
9. Let cool
10. Mix sour cream, cottage (or ricotta) cheese and sugar until creamy
11. Place 1 tablespoon of creamy mixture onto crepe
12. Roll up crepe with creamy filling inside
13. Top with fruit compote and whipped cream
14. ENJOY!

FEAST OF TRUMPETS[72]
(also NEW YEAR'S DAY or ROSH HASHANAH)

On the Jewish calendar: 1-2 *Tishrei* (September-October)

The LORD said to Moses, "Say to the Israelites: 'On the first day of the seventh month you are to have a day of rest, a sacred assembly commemorated with trumpet blasts. Do no regular work, but present an offering made to the LORD by fire.'"[73]

HOLIDAY BACKGROUND

Starting as a simple holiday, this day has become multi-faceted, taking on different meanings and significances that meet a variety of spiritual and community needs. The trumpet (or *shofar* [a modified ram or antelope's horn]) blasts fill this day, and this alone ushers in the solemnity that leads the nation into the Days of Awe and then *Yom Kippur*, the Day of Atonement.

The first (and second) days of the Jewish New Year are *Rosh Hashanah*, which means literally, head of the year. It is known as a time of

---

[72] *Rosh Hashanah* is the beginning of the "Jewish New Year" by tradition, since it is a time of annual repentance and has been the international beginning of the agricultural year before the giving of the *Torah*. This is not to be in conflict with *Nissan/ Aviv* (the official New Year mandated by God for the reference of time). However, *Rosh Hashanah,* in the month of *Tishrei*, was also kept and used for the calculation of Sabbath and Jubilee years.
[73] Leviticus 23:23-25

"loud blasts" and a day of remembrance, a type of memorial day as is evidence by Lev 23:24.[74] It is also referred to as the beginning of the aforementioned ten Days of Awe—a time for serious self-examination and meditation with a goal of repentance. This day is traditionally observed with joy and hope for the year ahead as well as the solemnity of self-reflection. For this is the time that the entire human race is said to be judged for the coming year. Each life is taken into account. It is this time that God determines whether or not each will be sealed in the Book of Life for the year.

An old child's book of verses recites a poem of *Rosh Hashanah* called, "The New Year:"

> No bells ring through the midnight air,
> No sound of vulgar revelry,
> But everywhere the trumpet blare
> Sends greetings over land and sea.
> And in the Jewish household reigns
> A quiet born of pious thought;
> And every Jewish heart attains
> A joy from festive fervor wrought.
> No ribald shout, no course display
> Proclaims our *Rosh Hashanah* here:
> But we who hope and smile and pray—
> In this wise greet the glad New Year (Burstein, 27).

This antiquated (yet appropriately valid) poem helps illustrate the solemnity of the day in contrast with other bawdy celebrations of the New Year by other cultures.

---

[74] The greatness of the day becomes even more pronounced around the time that the exile in Babylon was over in 6th century B.C.E. (Nehemiah 7:72-8:13).

CREATION [75]

This day is also traditionally attributed to the birthday of the world. According to rabbinic discussion, God is believed to have created humanity during this Creation week. Thus, this is to be enjoyed as the anniversary of humanity's beginning as well as God's sovereignty over all Creation. Each year on *Rosh Hashanah*, the Jewish nation proclaims God as the one true King.

According to Jewish tradition, many events are believed to have happened on this day aside from the six days of Creation as mentioned above. Upon this day, Abraham and Jacob had birthdays, Sarah, Rachel and Hannah finally conceived (Isaac, Joseph and Samuel respectively) in their previously-barren wombs. This is said to also have been the day Joseph had been released from the Egyptian prison. Tradition continues that upon this day was the binding of Isaac (when God commanded Abraham to sacrifice his son).[76] All these events are said to have occurred on *Rosh Hashanah*. [77]

BOOK OF LIFE

This is a solemn occasion allowing us to meditate upon the past year as well as to look ahead to the new year just beginning. Greetings are said to each other, "*La Shanah Tova Tikatavu!*" (May you be inscribed for a good year!) This is referring to the Book of Life in which we all hope to be sealed.

---

[75] Scripture does not state any link between *Rosh Hashanah* and either Creation or the "New Year," but this day has been attributed to it for spiritually symbolic reasons. Scripture mandates that the year officially must begin with the month containing Passover (*Nissan/ Aviv*), so the repentance of *Rosh Hashanah* may be better considered to be kicking off a "fiscal" year of repentance.
[76] Genesis 22:1-19
[77] Rabbi Eliezer as quoted in the B. Talmud, *Rosh Hashanah* 10b-11a

Although this is a time for self-contemplation and spiritual reflection, this is also a great time to enjoy the special aspects of the holiday. There is joy in knowing that the old is behind, and the new is ahead; a clean slate awaits.

TRADITIONAL OBSERVANCE

Beginning in the evening of when the holy day begins, the day is to be greeted with candles and blessings in the like manner of Sabbath. The day is a Sabbath as well, and thus is treated as one; the candles help mark the transition of the day from secular to holy.

CANDLES

The *Rosh Hashanah* blessing to be said over the candles is as follows:

> *Baruch ata Adonai, Eloheinu Melech ha-olam, asher kideshanu bemitzvotav vetzivanu lehadlik ner shel Yom Tov. (Amen).*

In English:

> **Blessed are You Lord our God, King of the universe, Who has sanctified us with His commandments and commanded us to kindle the festival lights. (Amen).**

Following this blessing, another, the *Shehecheyanu* is added in blessing God for bringing us to this holiday:

> *Baruch ata Adonai, Eloheinu Melech ha-olam, shehecheyanu vekiyenamu, vehigianu la'zeman hazeh. (Amen).*

In English:

Blessed are You Lord our God, King of the universe, Who gave us life, and sustains us, and enabled us to reach this season of joy. (Amen).

READINGS

The readings associated with the holiday are out of *Genesis*. The first story is of Hagar and Ishmael. When conflicts arose between Sarah and her Egyptian slave Hagar, the slave escapes by running headlong into the desert. Hagar, accompanied by her son Ishmael (fathered by Abraham), wandered aimlessly in the parched desert while frantically seeking water for herself and her young boy. She cried out to God who heard her voice and saved both her and the child, promising to make her son a father of a great nation and commanding her to return to Abraham and Sarah. God deals kindly with Hagar by showing her mercy and sustaining her in the desert.

The second reading is the story of the binding of Isaac. Abraham dearly loves his son of promise, Isaac. He is commanded to sacrifice Isaac upon an altar to God. Undoubtedly, grieved and devastated, Abraham nevertheless obeys. As Isaac lies bound upon the altar with his father's knife about to end his life, a heavenly voice suddenly halts Abraham and points him toward a ram that is caught in a nearby thicket. This animal becomes the sacrifice, the substitute for Isaac.

Both these stories are quite significant during *Rosh Hashanah*. These stories illustrate the struggle of humanity, the real-life issues that arise within families. Jealousy, contention and disregard often threaten to tear asunder the family unit—siblings, parents and children. *Rosh Hashanah* is the perfect time to both address and wrestle with these dilemmas, rediscovering the humility and limitations that encapsulate our human existence.

FRUITY CHALLAH

This is also the day of proclaiming the Kingship of God. The *challah* loaves are not baked like they normally are during other times of the year—such as braided and elongated or oval. The *Rosh Hashanah* loaves are made round or like spirals (similar to a cinnamon roll) ultimately to resemble a crown in commemoration of our God who is our King. The *challot* (plural for *challah*) are also baked with raisins or other extra sweet additions in celebration of the new year just beginning. Apples are a favorite *Rosh Hashanah* food—especially dipped in honey. Some dip their *challah* in sugar and only eat sweet foods during this time, since Judaism is rich with symbols, and the aim is to have a sweet New Year.

RAM OR ANTELOPE HORN (SHOFAR)

> *"The great shofar is sounded—and a still small voice is heard."*[78]

In the synagogue, the *shofar* is blown one hundred times.[79] Children particularly enjoy the *shofar*, and some rather contemporary-styled congregations encourage the children to join in on plastic ones after or during the ceremony. The service on this day invites all to a time of introspection and forgiveness—forgiveness of each other as well as forgiveness for ourselves. The *shofar* is intrinsically linked to this season of repentance.

Usually the *shofar* is a curved ram's horn in memory of the ram caught in the thicket that became the replacement for the sacrifice of Isaac. The Yemenite Jews, however, use a long antelope horn as their *shofar*. The *shofar* is a great and loud call to repentance. Anyone who has heard a *shofar*

---

[78] The *Machzor* holiday prayer book
[79] The *shofar* is not blown if *Rosh Hashanah* falls upon the seventh-day Sabbath.

blown properly can testify of its dreadful and awesome sound. The sound reaches to your depth and is a very appropriate means of bringing people to solemnity and repentance!

Saadia Gaon, a ninth century Babylonian scholar, taught that we are given ten reasons why we are obligated to sound the *shofar* on *Rosh Hashanah*:

> [1st reason]: Just as earthly kings have horns and trumpets blown to celebrate the anniversary of their coronation, so God wants the *shofar* blown on the anniversary of the Creation—when there came to be a world that God could rule over. [2nd reason]: Just as earthly kings have horns and trumpets blown to announce their decrees—and only after this warning actually enforce the decree—so God wants the *shofar* blown to announce the beginning of the Ten Days [of Awe], when all are commanded to turn their lives around. [3rd reason]: Just as the *shofar* blew when God gave the *Torah* at Mount Sinai, so it blows to remind us each year to do as our forebears said at Sinai: "We will act and we will hearken." [4th reason]: Just as Ezekiel compared the words of the prophets, calling for the people to change their ways, to a *shofar*—so we must know that those who hear the *shofar* and do not take warning and change our lives will be responsible for their own destruction. [5th reason]: Because the *shofar* was blown as a war-alarm when the Temple was destroyed, it should remind us of the destruction of the Temple—the disaster that we brought upon ourselves—and thus should warn us to abandon our misdeeds in order to avert disaster. [6th reason]: Because God used a ram as a substitute sacrifice for Isaac, the ram's horn should remind us how Isaac and Abraham were prepared to give up all their hopes and dreams for God's sake. [7th reason]: Since the blowing of a horn causes cities to tremble, so the *shofar* will make us tremble and fear our Creator. [8th reason]: Since the *shofar*

will be blown on the great Day of Judgment, blowing it now reminds us that every day is a day of judgment. [9th reason]: Since the *shofar* will be blown when the tempest-tossed of the Jewish people are gathered in harmony to the Land of Israel, we should hear the *shofar* to stir our longings for that day. [10th reason]: Since the *shofar* will be blown when the Messiah revives the dead, we hear the *shofar* in order to revive our faith in that supernatural transformation, the final victory of life and freedom over death, the ultimate oppressor (Waskow, 1982:16-17).

Thus, the unequaled call of the *shofar* has many significant connotations with remorse and repentance, thereby establishing itself as a perfect symbol of the occasion—a terrible sound that captures both the power and terror of divine reckoning as well as the sobbing and penitent wail of contrite repentance.

CASTING OFF (TASHLICH)

On the afternoon of the first day of *Rosh Hashanah*, a 'casting off,' commonly referred to as a *tashlich* ceremony is often performed.[80] Both during and after the Talmudic period (roughly 70-500 C.E.), this unique event became a popular way of making the abstract concept of "forgiveness of sins" into a better visualized concrete lesson. This ceremony usually takes place near a stream or flowing body of water (preferably with fish present). Different Jewish communities have embraced various ways of performing the *tashlich* ceremony. Fischer describes devout Jews emptying their pockets and tossing stones or bread into the water (Fischer, 2004: accessed 04 Aug 2010). This physical re-enactment of the forgiveness of sins through symbolism give the readings more force (usually involving visualizations of sin being swept away by water):

---

[80] Ashkenazi Jews do not perform this on the seventh-day Sabbath.

> *Kurdish Jews have actually leaped into the water and swam like fish to [symbolically] cleanse themselves of sin. Chassidim in Galicia sent little floats of straw out upon the water, set them afire with candles, and rejoiced that their sins were either burned up or washed away. In Jerusalem, where even brooks are hard to find,* tashlich *is done at a well (Waskow, 1982:19).*

The idea of sins being cleansed or "washed away" is better understood by both children and adults alike when such acts are performed. Watching something tossed into the water as it disappears, never to be seen again, illustrates the finality and permanence of divine forgiveness.

Water is also a powerful symbol in scripture, present throughout the creation of the world and during all stages of life. Not only was water the chosen medium chosen by God during the days of Noah by which to cleanse the earth, but it also often denotes themes of power, strength and might. True forgiveness involves these very virtues. This adds to its significance in the ceremony. In the most common *tashlich* practice, bread crumbs are brought to the water's edge. Often Psalms 130 is read:

> **Out of the depths I cry to you, O LORD;**
>
> **O Lord, hear my voice.**
> **Let Your ears be attentive**
> **to my cry for mercy.**
>
> **If You, O LORD, kept a record of sins,**
> **O Lord, who could stand?**
>
> **But with You there is forgiveness;**
> **therefore You are feared.**
>
> **I wait for the LORD, my soul waits,**
> **and in His word I put my hope.**

> My soul waits for the Lord
> more than watchmen wait for the morning,
>
> O Israel, put your hope in the LORD,
> for with the LORD is unfailing love
> and with Him is full redemption.
>
> He Himself will redeem Israel
> from all their sins.[81]

Following this reading, a prayer is given, and the bread crumbs are cast into the water. This is to symbolize casting off sins into the depths of oblivion. The fish also set upon the crumbs, devouring them, ensuring their disappearance. Sometimes, especially with young children, the specific faults and sins are named (such as lying, disobedience, being disrespectful, etc.) as the crumbs are tossed into the water. This helps the children visualize their wrongs being forgiven and forgotten. This method of making the intangible a bit more solid for children and adults alike can create a better understanding of what it is like to be absolved so that a new beginning can commence in accordance to the prophet Micah:

> He will take us back in love;
>
> He will cover up our iniquities.
>
> You will cast all their sins into the depths of the sea.[82]

JESUS IN THE FEAST OF TRUMPETS (YESHUA IN ROSH HASHANAH)

Yeshua is at the center of this holiday. He is the Christian King of Kings, the Messianic and Heavenly conqueror. The blowing of the *shofarot* (plural

---

[81] Psalm 130:1-8
[82] Micah 7:19

for *shofar*) is a sign of the return of this Messianic King. Christian paintings illustrate scenes which often depict the Second Coming of the Lord as having the heavenly host surrounding the coming King while blowing trumpets. "When the trump shall sound..." goes the prophecy of the Second Advent. Believers await the coming of the Messiah in such a manner, a euphoric scene filled with trumpets and their blasts. Initially, silver trumpets were used; however, these came to be replaced by the *shofar*.

As explained earlier, the *shofar* is a symbol of the ram caught in the bush which became Isaac's replacement. The metaphor is heightened when further symbolism comes to play; Isaac is the representation of Yeshua:

> **By faith Abraham, when he was tried, offered up Isaac: and he that received the promises offered up his only begotten son, Of whom it was said, That in Isaac shall thy seed be called: Accounting that God was able to raise him up, even from the dead; from whence also he received him in a figure.**[83]

Both were born of miracle births and then obedient to the point of sacrifice. Just as Abraham was told to offer up his heir on the altar, so God Himself had to offer up His own son.

The symbolism does not end here. Trumpets and *shofarot* are also signals of war. Yeshua came first as a humble baby. Yeshua will come again in the clouds as a king of the army of God. Yeshua came first to defeat the hold of sin on humanity while planting seeds to ready the world for its ultimate deliverance; He will come again, and this time as the awaited Messiah warrior to defeat the powers of darkness.

HOW CAN THIS BENEFIT YOU, A CHRISTIAN?

Christians battle the unseen foe. The battlefield is drawn, and the Christian finds himself/herself quite positively within its boundaries.

---

[83] Hebrews 11:17-19

Rosh Hashanah, a day filled with *shofar* blasts and the call to wage spiritual warfare is just the opportunity to ensure that he/she is on the winning side! Although the battle belongs to the Lord, the Christian often finds himself/herself in the very midst of it. We can identify with the opportunity to take up our spiritual armor and war against evil. Paul wrote:

> ***Put on the full armor of God so that you can take your stand against the devil's schemes. For our struggle is not against flesh and blood, but against the rulers, against the authorities, against the powers of this dark world and against the spiritual forces of evil In the heavenly realms. Therefore put on the full armor of God, so that when the day of evil comes, you may be able to stand your ground, and after you have done everything, to stand.*** [84]

Rosh Hashanah can be a very spiritually significant time for Christians. This is an opportunity for repentance, forgiveness and reflection. Many believe in God, but that is not enough, for even Satan believes in Him. This is discussed in scripture: "You believe that there is one God. Good! Even the demons believe that—and shudder."[85] So, more than simple belief is required of us in our walk. We need to repent and be in total submission and sincerity in our request for that forgiveness made available to use through the sacrifice of this, our Messiah, our King of Kings. This is a perfect opportunity to begin to search deep within ourselves. This is the day our Savior is waiting to renew our walk with Him. This is a day of the Jewish New Year, and thus it is a good time for new beginnings. Why not begin anew with the Savior?

---

[84] Ephesians 6:11-13
[85] James 2:19

HOLIDAY NOSHES (SNACKS)

Here's to a *sweet* New Year! This day is usually celebrated with sweet foods. Traditionally, apple slices are eaten with honey. Also, the *Rosh Hashanah challah*, as mentioned, is made round like a crown and made with the added sweetness of raisins. The previous *challah* recipe would work for this, except remember to add a 3/4 cup of raisins to the dough. You can add other dried fruit as well. Add this nice *challah* to some honey-dipped apple slices (tart varieties are best with the honey, or so our family thinks). Here is a great recipe to begin the new year. The sweetness is needed to help balance all the solemnity of the day (and next ten).

ROSH HASHANAH APPLE BUNDT (pareve)

Ingredients

- 1 cup brown sugar
- 1/2 cup vegetable oil
- 2 eggs
- 3/4 cup honey
- 1 teaspoon vanilla extract (optional)
- 2 1/2 cups all-purpose flour
- 1 teaspoon baking powder
- 1 teaspoon baking soda
- 1 teaspoon salt
- 2 teaspoon ground cinnamon
- 1/4 teaspoon ground allspice
- 3 tart apples - peeled, cored and grated
- 1 cup chopped nuts (walnuts, almonds or pecans)

Variation

- 3/4 cup red cinnamon candy can be added for a nice red color and cinnamon flavor. Simply reduce cinnamon to 1/2 teaspoon and reduce sugar to 3/4 cup.

Directions

1. Preheat the oven to 325 degrees F
2. Grease and flour a 9 inch Bundt pan
3. In a large bowl, stir together the sugar and oil.
4. Beat in the eggs until light, then stir in the honey and vanilla
5. Combine the flour, baking powder, baking soda, salt, cinnamon and allspice
6. Stir into the batter just until moistened
7. Fold in the apples and nuts (and candy if desired).
8. Bake for 50 to 65 minutes in the preheated oven, or until a toothpick inserted into the crown comes out clean.
9. Let cool for 10 to 15 minutes before inverting onto a plate (and tapping out of the pan)
10. Garnish with apple slices when cooled
11. Dribble with thin streams of honey or dust with powdered sugar if desired
12. ENJOY!

ROSH HASHANAH SPICE COOKIES (pareve)

Ingredients

- 1/2 cup margarine
- 1 1/3 cups packed brown sugar
- 1 egg

- 2 cups all purpose flour
- 1 teaspoon baking soda
- 1/2 teaspoon salt
- 1 teaspoon ground cinnamon
- 1 teaspoon ginger
- 1/4 teaspoon ground nutmeg
- 1/8 teaspoon ground cloves
- 1 cup apples (peeled, cored, diced)
- 1 cup raisins or chopped dates
- 3/4 cup apple sauce
- 1 1/2 cups sifted powdered sugar
- 1/2 teaspoon vanilla extract
- 2 1/2 Tablespoons grated orange zest

Variation

- 1/2 cup chopped nuts (pecans, walnuts or almonds)

Directions

1. Preheat oven 400 F
2. Beat margarine and brown sugar together until light and fluffy
3. Beat in egg and blend thoroughly
4. Stir together flour, baking soda, salt, cinnamon, cloves, ginger and nutmeg
5. Combine half of the dry ingredients into creamed mixture
6. Mix together the nuts, apple, raisins, remaining half of dry ingredients and apple sauce
7. Drop from tablespoon 1 1/2 inches apart onto lightly greased baking sheet

8. Bake for 10-12 minutes
9. Remove cookies to racks while still warm
10. Spread or drizzle with glaze
11. To make Glaze: Combine powdered sugar, margarine, vanilla and enough cream to make glaze of spreading or drizzling consistency. Beat until smooth. Spread or drizzle (depending upon desired consistency) on warm cookies
12. ENJOY!

DAYS OF AWE (YAMIM NORAIM)

On the Jewish calendar: 1 Tishrei-10 Tishrei (September-October)

HOLIDAY BACKGROUND

During the ten days following *Rosh Hashanah*, we are in a state of examining ourselves. These days are called the "Days of Awe" or *Aseret Yemei Teshuvah* (Days of Repentance). We are invited to use these days to closely examine our behavior from the previous year to repent of wrongdoing. Jewish tradition holds that people are in three categories: 1. righteous, 2. wicked, and 3. *beinoni* (those in between). Those who are *beinoni* are advised to use this time to tip the scales in their favor, to make their paths straight.

TRADITIONAL OBSERVANCE

During this time of repentance, all have the opportunity to right the wrongs in life to better serve God as His people. Some people pray more during this time and others fast in sincere repentance and make choices in their lives so that they are in line with *Torah*, or God's instructions.

HOW CAN THIS BENEFIT YOU, A CHRISTIAN?

Some might see this as legalism; however, even in these actions, the penitent Jew knows that he/she is ultimately saved solely by the grace of

God. If we love God, we keep His commands. This is a beneficial time for Christians to ensure that all are right with Him and to demonstrate our love for our Redeemer by keeping our end of the divine covenant as God's people. As followers of Yeshua, our lives are fraught with trials, temptations and hardships. Often, in the rush, hustle, and bustle of life, we do not examine ourselves and our own motives. Often we make decisions in haste and may forget to acknowledge God's way. We may not make the most prudent choices in life. This is a great time to reassess all the details of our lives to ensure that we are living for God so that no sin can creep into our lives. Repentance is liberating! This span of ten days is the perfect time to experience this freedom. We started the process on *Rosh Hashanah*, so let's continue these ten more days.

DAY OF ATONEMENT (YOM KIPPUR)

On the Jewish calendar: 10 Tishrei (September-October)

Once a year Aaron shall make atonement.... This annual atonement must be made with the blood of the atoning sin offering for the generations to come. It is most holy to the LORD.[86]

This is to be a lasting ordinance for you: On the tenth day of the seventh month you must deny yourselves and not do any work— whether native-born or an alien living among you- because on this day atonement will be made for you, to cleanse you. Then, before the LORD, you will be clean from all your sins.[87]

The tenth day of this seventh month is the Day of Atonement. Hold a sacred assembly and deny yourselves, and present an offering made to the LORD by fire.[88]

Then have the trumpet sounded everywhere on the tenth day of the seventh month; on the Day of Atonement sound the trumpet throughout your land.[89]

---

[86] Exodus 30:10
[87] Leviticus 16:29-30
[88] Leviticus 23:27
[89] Leviticus 25:9

On the tenth day of this seventh month hold a sacred assembly. You must deny yourselves and do no work. [90]

HISTORICAL BACKGROUND

This day is mentioned several times in the *Torah*. The significance of the day is quite apparent as the Sabbath of Sabbaths, the "Day of Redemption" or even "Day of Judgment." If *Rosh Hashanah* is a day of self-assessment, meditation and renewal, of accounting of the soul and beginning adjustments in our attitudes and behavior starting the following solemn ten Days of Awe, then *Yom Kippur* is the culmination of these ten days of reflection. This is the day of the Jewish calendar in which the sin of the nation was transferred and atoned for. Once a year, the nation would come together for a time of cleansing, fasting, reflecting and solemnly contemplating the righteousness of God. Also, this day is referred to in the *Torah* as the *Shabbat Shabbaton,* or Sabbath of Sabbaths. This does not mean it was an ultimate rest day or a period of supreme restfulness even greater than the weekly Sabbath. In fact, the term simply refers to the sheer holiness of the day. This is a day like no other in the Hebrew year. This is a day for us to ensure that our spiritual slate is clean, a time to purge our hearts with repentance and our bodies with fasting. This is the most serious and somber day of the year. Our instruction comes from Leviticus, "… In the seventh month, on the tenth day of the month, you shall afflict your souls." [91] This date is represented in the Jewish calendar as the tenth of *Tishri*. In the times of the Temple in Jerusalem, *Yom Kippur* was the most important time of year. The high priest would spend the previous ten days studying all of the rituals and steps he was required to perform. This is the day when he would enter the most holy place, the Holy of Holies, to make atonement for the nation.

---

[90] Numbers 29:7
[91] Leviticus 16:29-31

This was a very solemn day for the priest. He would don new attire for this day. He would put on four white garments of flax (linen). He would wear a golden crown on his forehead and a breastplate on his heart. He would put on an external garment decorated with pomegranates and bells on the hem.[92] An apron or vest was worn on top of this. He also had a belt, turban and pants.[93] The priest was to be well-covered on this holy day, coming before the Lord with his nakedness well hidden. The priest would offer a bull as a sin offering for himself and the priesthood before filling the censor with live coals from the altar. He would burn incense on these coals in the Holy of Holies. He made more burnt offerings: seven male yearling lambs, a young bull, and a ram. A male goat comprised the sin offering (all male animals were used here). The *Mishnah*, a literary Jewish supplement, describes these priestly duties. The rituals were many, and each required detailed accuracy. The sacred name of God[94] was uttered ten times while all the people bowed in reverence. With everything taken into account, the priest was to make over forty trips between the court and the sanctuary on this day. Each and every move was carefully planned and deliberate.[95] Mistakes, improper cleansing, or inattention to detail could result in the death of the priest (thus the aforementioned bells on his hem to give evidence of his movement in the Holy of Holies, proof to those outside that he was not dead).

After the purification of the Holy Place and tending to the altar of burnt offerings, the High Priest took two goats. One goat was for God, and one was for *Azazel* (the scapegoat). Two tablets of stone with the words for each were shuffled and then put in front of the goats. The tablet saying "for God" indicated that the goat by it must be sacrificed. The tablet saying "for *Azazel*" indicated that the goat was to be the scapegoat

---

[92] The bells were put on his hem so that the people could hear them ringing, giving evidence that the priest was still alive upon entering into the Holy of Holies.
[93] Leviticus 8:7; Exodus 28:33-35
[94] *Yod-Hey-Vav-Hey*, also known as the *tetragrammaton*, is so sacred that it has fallen into disuse and has been forgotten
[95] Yoma 3:4-8:9.

carrying off the sins of the nation upon his head. It was upon the head of the latter that the priest would confess the sins of the nation before it was released and chased into the wilderness:

> *Then he is to take the two goats and present them before the LORD at the entrance to the Tent of Meeting. He is to cast lots for the two goats—one lot for the LORD and the other for the scapegoat. Aaron shall bring the goat whose lot falls to the LORD and sacrifice it for a sin offering. But the goat chosen by lot as the scapegoat shall be presented alive before the LORD to be used for making atonement by sending it into the desert as a scapegoat.*[96]

The two goats represented different things. One died for God immediately, and one lived with the sin upon his head but was shooed into the desert. Of this scapegoat, it continues:

> *Then he shall come out to the altar that is before the LORD and make atonement for it. He shall take some of the bull's blood and some of the goat's blood and put it on all the horns of the altar. The goat will carry on itself all their sins to a solitary place; and the man shall release it in the desert.*[97]

The scapegoat was released into the desert as described, not to be retrieved again. Along with this tradition was that of tying a red sash on the horns of the scapegoat as well as upon the outer door of the Temple. Both of the red sashes (or cords) were monitored and then reported as to whether they had changed to white or if they had stayed the same crimson color.

---

[96] Leviticus 16:7-10
[97] Leviticus 16:18-22

"Come now, let us reason together," says the LORD. "Though your sins are like scarlet, they shall be as white as snow; though they are red as crimson, they shall be like wool."[98]

Thus, with the red-to-white imagery prominent in the minds of the priests, there was much rejoicing when the cord turned white, however the priests were filled with sadness and shame if it did not transform at all. This implied that the sins of the nation remained.

Interestingly, the Talmud itself speaks of a time when the red cord ceased turning white altogether. "The Rabbis taught that forty years prior to the destruction of the Temple the lot did not come up in the [high priest's] right hand nor did the tongue of scarlet wool become white..." When we consider that the Temple was destroyed 70 C.E., then forty years prior would be around 30 C.E., which would coincide with the death of Yeshua.[99]

TRADITIONAL OBSERVANCE

Leading up to *Yom Kippur*, much preparation takes place, both in spiritual and physical worlds. During the Ten Days of Awe, self-examination has taken place. God does not automatically forgive us of our unaddressed interpersonal wrongs, so we must first apologize and seek forgiveness of those we may have hurt or wronged in the previous year. Also physically, we prepare ourselves for the affliction of our souls as we seek the forgiveness of our sins from our gracious Creator. We fast during the day and night of *Yom Kippur*, so we feast prior to opening the day (late afternoon, early evening before sundown). Many spend most of the day in the synagogue attending five prayer services with the evening one being the most prominent *Yom Kippur* service, *Kol Nidre*. Like most Jewish holidays, charity is prominent on this day of *Yom Kippur*. Many Jews will not say "no" to charitable requests upon this day.

---

[98] Isaiah 1:18
[99] talmud Tractate Yoma 39b

CANDLES

We light candles prior to *Yom Kippur* as we do on *Shabbat* with the *Yom Kippur* blessing followed by the *Shehecheyanu*, the blessing for the new season (as previously demonstrated for *Rosh Hashanah*). Traditionally, three candles may be used instead of the customary two. The third is to be in commemoration of our loved ones that have passed on before us as a tribute to their memory. "The lifebreath of man (*neshamah*) is the lamp (*ner*) of the Lord"[100] (Steinburg, 2007:75). This candle is optional. The blessing said over the *Yom Kippur* candles as the holiday is greeted as follows:

> *Baruch ata Adonai, Eloheinu Melech ha-olam, asher kideshanu bemitzvotav vetzivanu lehadlik ner shel Shel Yom Ha-Kippurim. (Amen).*[101]

In English:

> **Blessed are You, Lord our God, King of the universe, who has sanctified us with His commandments, and commanded us to kindle the light of the Day of Atonement. (Amen).**

The *Shechechanu* is also said as it is on all special occasions:

> *Baruch ata Adonai, Eloheinu Melech ha-olam, shehecheyanu vekiyenamu, vehigianu la'zeman hazeh. (Amen).*

In English:

> **Blessed are You Lord our God, King of the universe, Who gave us life, and sustains us, and enabled us to reach this season of joy. (Amen).**

---

[100] Proverbs 20:27
[101] *Yom Kippur* here appears in its plural form as it does in Rabbinic literature.

CLOTHING AND ADORNMENT

Self-denial is a prominent theme of this day. Scripture admonishes the Jewish people to "afflict" themselves. We interpret this as fasting and refraining from luxury or merriment. Leather footwear is discarded in favor of shoes of canvas or other non-leather materials, as leather is traditionally a sign of luxury. Lotions, perfumes and women's cosmetics are not worn this day, and washing past the knuckles is not commonly permitted. There are varying customs as to what should be worn. Depending upon the community, it might be traditional to wear white. Men in some communities wear a white *kittel* (a gown / robe to be worn during their burial). Also, *talliot*, or prayer shawls, are often worn all day—despite the usual custom to only wear them only during daylight hours. Personally, I like to wear white on *Yom Kippur*, as it is a very appropriate metaphor of purity and forgiveness of sins and is worn in commemoration of the text saying that our sins are to be made *white* as mentioned previously in the context of the transformation of the scarlet sash.[102] Thusly, and for this reason also, white is popular among the more conservative traditions. I went to a different and more progressive congregation one year, and you can imagine my surprise when I noticed they all wore black for sobriety. I was more than a little conspicuous in my white attire! Judaism is not static; it is dynamic. Though incomplete without the acceptance of Yeshua, the rightful Messiah, Judaism is not dead, but seems to live and breathe on its very own. Therefore, it is important to realize that as consistent as the details in Jewish tradition may seem (as many are unchanged over millennia), uniqueness in interpretation and expression can also be very strong aspects of Judaism!

FASTING

Self-deprivation is not popular in the Western World, especially in America. In a society often given over unto indulgence, fasting is often treated as a torture. Elliot Dorff explains:

---

[102] Isaiah 1:18

Fasting and services all day long. That, unfortunately, is all that comes to mind when most Jews think of *Yom Kippur*, the Day of Atonement. It is definitely a "downer" and flies in the face of what American culture has taught us to value—namely, individual freedom and happiness (Steinburg, 2007:99).

This fact makes *Yom Kippur* all the more relevant to those of us who need to pull away from our everyday indulgences to pause for introspection. This occasion of sobriety and temporary deprivation contrasts most sharply with our lives of first-world culinary decadence, thereby making the season of repentance all the more poignant.

The fasting and self-affliction of Jews on *Yom Kippur* may be grossly misunderstood by the foreign observer. The ritual may seem to be legalistic or in line with the penance of Catholicism. On the contrary, Steinburg explains,

> God wants us to fast as a means to improve ourselves, not simply to suffer.... Self-denial, specifically of the fast, functions as an emotional and spiritual form of expiation, which will lead to our better behavior... Abstinence as practiced in Judaism differs distinctly and importantly from that of other religions. Classic Catholicism, for example teaches that one should suppress and over power physical desires, while Judaism teaches that we should repress and consciously set bounds on them (2007:75).

Therefore, the fasting and affliction of self on *Yom Kippur* are, in effect, methods of achieving a meditative contemplation and prayer so as to elevate the spirituality above the ordinary realms of daily living. There is no benefit in Judaism for penance on *Yom Kippur*, but instead an invitation for self-improvement and a transformation of the mind from the base and common to the holy and spiritual.

Why do we opt for this physical fasting and self-denial in our observance? Why can we not choose simply a spiritual or inward affliction of self? Religions such as Catholicism teach that one should have mind and spirit overpower physical or "animalistic" desires. This comes from a Gnostic understanding of the body and flesh as corrupt. With the idea that the body is the epitome of sin, with only the spirit containing the potential for righteousness, the denial of the physical is seen as an act of empowering the spirit—as the body and spirit are separate weights on opposing sides of the scale. Judaism takes a different view. The Talmud concurs, "The Holy Blessed One takes the soul, throws it into the body, and judges them as one"[103] Judaism understands body and soul as a complete entity (Steinburg, 2007:75).

READINGS

Sin and Confession
We have sinned against You purposely and by mistake...
We have sinned against You by speaking badly of others...
We have sinned against You by greed and oppressive interest
We have sinned against You by rashly judging others...
For all these sins, forgiving God, forgive us, pardon us,
Grant us atonement.

Ve-al kulam Elo-ha selichot, selach lanu,
Mechal lanu, kaper lanu
--The *Al Het* Confessoinal, High Holiday *Machzor* (Steinburg, 2007:90).

Isaiah's Fast
Is such the fast I desire,
A day for men to starve their bodies?
Is it bowing the head like a bulrush

---

[103] Talmud, *Sukkah* 53a.

And lying in sackcloth and ashes?
Do you call that a fast?
A day when the LORD is favorable?
No, this is the fast I desire:
To unlock fetters of wickedness,
And untie the cords of the yoke
To let the oppressed go free;
To break off every yoke.
It is to share your bread with the hungry,
And to take the wretched poor into your home;
When you see the naked, to clothe him,
And not to ignore your own kin.
Then shall your light burst through like the dawn
And your healing spring up quickly.[104]

JESUS IN THE DAY OF ATONEMENT
(YESHUA IN YOM KIPPUR)

With Yeshua at the very heart of our redemption from sin, he is the central figure of this holiday. How did Yeshua fulfill this special day? Richard Booker explains:

> [He] fulfilled the spiritual aspects of the Day of Atonement when He went into the heavenly Holy of Holies with His own blood He shed for the sins of the world. Believers have been forgiven and made clean once and for all by the blood of Messiah.... (Booker, 2009:127).

Just as the High Priest labored for the atoning of the sins of the nation, so our Messiah, our own High Priest works to purify us so that we can have fellowship with him and the Father. Just as the High

---

[104] Isaiah 58:5-8

Priest was to go behind the veil into the Holy of Holies and sprinkle the blood of the sacrificial offering onto the Mercy Seat, so our Messiah shed his own blood and likewise cleanses us from sin—not for just the year but for all time. He does this so that we may stand blameless before the Father.

The Messiah had been established as the new High Priest for his people through the events that occurred during Passover (his death, resurrection and ascension) and is thus now making intercession for us all. The believer does not have to stand afar as in these ancient times before the sacrifice of our Savior. We each have direct access to God through our High Priest and Messiah and can approach the throne of grace. How did our Savior accomplish this?

> ***When Christ came as high priest of the good things that are already here, he went through the greater and more perfect Tabernacle that is not man-made, that is to say, not a part of this creation. He did not enter by means of the blood of goats and calves; but he entered the Most Holy Place once [and] for all by his own blood, having obtained eternal redemption. The blood of goats and bulls and the ashes of a heifer sprinkled on those who are ceremonially unclean sanctify them so that they are outwardly clean. How much more, then, will the blood of Christ, who through the eternal Spirit offered himself unblemished to God, cleanse our consciences from acts that lead to death, so that we may serve the living God!*[105]**

The Tabernacle of the *Torah* was a great illustration of how sin prevented our connection, or access, to God. Just as the High Priest had to be purified and cleansed before he entered the Holy of Holies to escape death itself, our heavenly High Priest had to live a sinless life and present

---

[105] Hebrews 9:11-14

himself as pure to the throne of God. As the Tabernacle's system purified the flesh of the nation, so our heavenly High Priest cleanses us inwardly. This is where the blood of bulls and goats cannot help us. The earthly Tabernacle rituals on *Yom Kippur* were to remind the nation that perfect atonement had not yet been made, as the earthly ceremony foreshadowed it and pointed to it. Thus our Messiah, Yeshua, became the atoning sacrifice for the whole world, redeeming us from death and restoring us evermore.

More Messianic significance abounds, explains Fischer, "atonement" (*Kippur*) means "ransom by means of a substitute." Yeshua was that substitute sacrificed for the sins of the world. *Oz M'lifnai* is a Musaf prayer found in older versions of the *Machzor*. It speaks in a manner that is Messianic in its terms and description of the Messiah and his role. This accurately describes Yeshua, the Christian's Jesus Christ:

> The Messiah our righteousness has turned from us. We are alarmed, we have no one to justify us. Our sins and the yoke of our transgressions he bore. He was bruised for our iniquities. He carried on his shoulders our sins. With his stripes we are healed. Almighty God, hasten the day that he might come to us anew; that we may hear from Mt. Lebanon a second time through the Messiah (Fischer, 2004: accessed 04 Aug 2010)

This holiday looks forward to the time when Israel will accept the atonement made by the Messiah—that atonement made not only for them, but for the entire earth.

HOW CAN THIS BENEFIT YOU, A CHRISTIAN?

As followers of Yeshua, we know that our sins are covered by the blood of our Savior. We know he has made the atonement for us through his death. Just because he died for us, are we above remorse for our wrongdoing?

We can still benefit from an ongoing cleansing in our lives. The dirt and shame of life in this world often cling to our garments. This is a time providing a perfect opportunity to shake it off.

Unlike most, the Jewish culture greets its New Year with introspection instead of revelry. There is plenty of time for joy and celebration once one is right with God and his/her fellows. Thus, the year is greeted solemnly. This is a lesson for Christians. While we have much to be merry about, and we rejoice over our salvation often, there is still merit in such gravity. The words of Ecclesiastes remind us of what often would contradict conventional opinions:

> A good name is better than fine perfume and the day of death better than the day of birth. It is better to go to a house of mourning than to go to a house of feasting, for death is the destiny of every man; the living should take this to heart. Sorrow is better than laughter, because a sad face is good for the heart.[106]

We are never beyond the requirement of solemnity and sobriety—and ultimately, repentance. This day reminds us to take the time to reflect and embrace anew the atoning sacrifice of our Savior. Often, when life is going well and easy, we do not think of repentance. Sometimes, only when hardships come our way do we take time to examine our lives before God. God does not bring the sorrows and hardships, but often He uses them for our good, to guide us in the right direction—and often this direction is one of self-examination and contrition. Yeshua often drew the hearts of his listeners to the invitation of humility and repentance. Prominent is his parable of the religious Pharisee and the sinful tax collector:

---

[106] Ecclesiastes 7:1-3

To some who were confident of their own righteousness and looked down on everybody else, Jesus told this parable: "Two men went up to the Temple to pray, one a Pharisee and the other a tax collector. The Pharisee stood up and prayed about himself: 'God, I thank you that I am not like other men—robbers, evildoers, adulterers—or even like this tax collector. I fast twice a week and give a tenth of all I get.' But the tax collector stood at a distance. He would not even look up to Heaven, but beat his breast and said, 'God, have mercy on me, a sinner.' I tell you that this man, rather than the other, went home justified before God. For everyone who exalts himself will be humbled, and he who humbles himself will be exalted."[107]

Here, Yeshua is demonstrating the virtue of humility and a penitent heart. The Pharisee was truly upright in his fasting twice a week. He was in the right to give a tenth of all he owned. He went to the Temple to pray out of a devotion and passion that was most likely sincere. The Pharisee was not doing wrong by his actions, as he was following the commandments of God—and then some. Yeshua used the Pharisee as a subject for his parable, not because Pharisees were necessarily corrupt, but because the opposite was known to be true. The parable loses the intended irony if the protagonist is a baddie from the beginning. It was none of his actions that incriminated him; it was solely his attitude. It was his lack of self-examination. His overconfidence in his righteousness is what brought him lower than the tax collector who was aware of his own shortcomings and admitted dependence upon the graciousness of God.

This is a perfect time to stop and reassess our lives. Fasting and praying in solemnity is not a bad idea! This is an opportunity to repent and renew our walk with our Messiah. This day, *Yom Kippur*, the day of afflicting our souls, is the perfect time to come before him with a humble

---

[107] Luke 18:13

attitude. Forget about the many good deeds we perform or the commandments we keep; today is about humbly recognizing our need for our Savior's cleansing. This day we need to don his righteousness so that we can come before the Heavenly throne.

We can also take our focus from ourselves and remember to pray on behalf of others. Fischer adds, "we can celebrate *Yom Kippur* by thanking God for the atonement available through Yeshua and by praying that more of our people will recognize and accept Him as their atonement" (Fischer, 2004: accessed 04 Aug 2010). This gives us a dual focus: we can be thankful for 1., our own sakes that we have this atonement for our sins while 2., praying for those around us who have yet to take and embrace this atonement for themselves.

HOLIDAY NOSHES (SNACKS)

Although *Yom Kippur* is a time of fasting, a good light dish is needed to break the fast. After having an empty stomach for a day, a meal simply digested is best. Here is a nice fruit salad that makes a perfect break for the fast.

HOLY LAND FRUIT SALAD (pareve)

Ingredients

- 2 oranges, peeled
- 2 apples
- 1 nectarine or peach
- 1 pomegranate
- 1 cup of grapes
- 1 12-18 oz. can cubed pineapple, drained
- 6 dates, chopped
- 1/2 cup of shredded masticated coconut

- 1/2 cup raisins
- 1/2 cup berries (strawberries, blueberries, blackberries, or boysenberries)

Variation

- 1/2 cup nuts or seeds may be added (any variety)

Directions

1. Drain can of pineapple, saving juice
2. Soak raisins in juice, set aside
3. Core and dice apples, peel oranges, pit nectarine / peach
4. Slice grapes in half lengthwise and toss with other chopped fruit including drained pineapple, whole berries, soaked (drained) raisins, coconut, dates and nuts if desired.
5. ENJOY!

FEAST OF TABERNACLES (OR BOOTHS) (SUKKOT)

On the Jewish calendar: 15 *Tishrei* (September-October)

The LORD said to Moses, "Say to the Israelites: 'On the fifteenth day of the seventh month, the LORD's Feast of Tabernacles begins, and it lasts for seven days. The first day is a sacred assembly; do no regular work. For seven days present offerings made to the LORD by fire .... After you have gathered the crops of the land, celebrate the festival to the LORD .... This is to be a lasting ordinance for the generations to come....[108]

Three times a year you are to celebrate a festival to me..... Celebrate the Feast of Harvest [also Tabernacles] with the first fruits of the crops you sow in your field. Celebrate the Feast of Ingathering at the end of the year, when you gather in your crops from the field.[109]

---

[108] Leviticus 23:33-43
[109] Exodus 23:14-16

The Feast of Tabernacles is also uniquely mentioned in what most Christians today classify as the *Parousia*, or predicted events surrounding the Second Coming of the Messiah:

> *Then the survivors from all the nations that have attacked Jerusalem will go up year after year to worship the King, the LORD Almighty, and to celebrate the Festival of Tabernacles. If any of the peoples of the earth do not go up to Jerusalem to worship the King, the LORD Almighty, they will have no rain.… This will be the punishment of … of all the nations that do not go up to celebrate the Festival of Tabernacles.*[110]

HOLIDAY BACKGROUND

One of the best holidays of the year, according to my children, is *Sukkot* (but then again, I am catching on to the idea that they are considering most of these holidays their "favorite" for one aspect or another). *Sukkot* is a holiday period beginning five days after *Yom Kippur* and typically lasting eight days (including the combined holidays of *Shemini Atzeret* and *Simchat Torah*).[111] This is a joyous festival to mark the end of the heavy sobriety of *Yom Kippur* as well as the hard toils of harvest. It was definitely a celebration and time of giving thanks. In fact, it is widely believed and argued that the American tradition of Thanksgiving came from this holiday via the religious Puritan settlers who appreciated Biblical holidays and banned "pagan" holidays such as Christmas. In the early Israelite nation, thanks went up to God for their abundance as they stored away the food for the winter while they prayed for rain and a good harvest in the coming year. Canaanites also had a great celebration at the end of the harvest, as many cultures did to revel in the completion of the agricultural labors of the year; however with Israel, it was something greater. Not

---

[110] Zechariah 14:16-18
[111] Some communities separate *Shimini Atzeret* and *Simchat Torah*, making the *Sukkot* holiday period nine days long.

only was the good harvest celebrated, but equally celebrated was the less illustrious theme of the forty years of wandering (camping) in the wilderness when no permanent homes had been erected, but only temporary dwellings—during the nomadic period of their post-Egypt history.

All in all, this was the merriest time of the year causing the land to ring with song and laughter. This was a pilgrimage holiday like Passover and *Shavuot*, meaning all Jewish people were required to be present at the sanctuary (and in later times, the Temple) for the celebration. They would all pour in from the Diaspora (after the establishment of Jerusalem) for this time of rejoicing. The solemnity of the previous holidays was to be balanced with the joy and celebration of a completed harvest and remembrance of their sojourn in the wilderness. As with human nature, sometimes the partying was overdone. Not surprisingly, however, this lack of moderation in the holiday's observance provoked the righteous:

> Amos visited the Temple at Beth-El during this festival. [The festivities and wild abandon of the people so abhorred him that he] condemned the sanctuary and the entire ritual of the festival. Hosea…also protested against the bacchanalia of the autumn festival…. Isaiah, who was a prophet in Jerusalem, tells us that all, even priests and prophets, were drunk in the sanctuary (Schauss, 1975:173).

Fortunately, not all celebrations were so out of control. Despite the occasions of excess, it was still considered a bigger travesty to under-celebrate than to over-celebrate. Even in its more conservative tones, it was definitely a time of rejoicing. Scripture tells us of the daughters of Shiloh celebrating in a more honorable way with dances to God as was appropriate during their time:

> In the very old days, before the founding of the Jewish kingdom, the most noted sanctuary was at Shiloh on Mount Ephraim, and we are told in the Book of Judges that the daughters of

Shiloh would hold a dance procession in the vineyards in honor of the Festival of God (Schauss, 1975:172).

Pilgrims from Ephraim such as these would bring their sacrifices to the sanctuary and eat them there as thanksgiving offerings (a thanksgiving dinner in it most literal form). Schauss states that Samuel's father Elkanah came here with Hannah and the rest of the family for the ritual celebration as well (1975:173).

TRADITIONAL OBSERVANCE

This is another Jewish holiday rich in imagery and hands-on fun. Come to think of it, most of them are. Most, if not all, Jewish holidays involve some kind of charity, and this holiday is no different. *Sukkot* observance encourages hospitality (to guests both real and imaginary). This was always a very joyous holiday, and today, the merriment continues.

CANDLES

Like most of all the Jewish holidays, *Sukkot* is welcomed with lighting candles, as have been the previously discussed holidays. Unlike the Sabbath candles, this time we say the blessing first with the candle lighting second. This is done in the *sukkah* (explained later). The blessing is as follows:

> ***Baruch ata Adonai, Eloheinu Melech ha-olam, asher kideshanu bemitzvotav vetzivanu lehadlik ner shel Yom Tov. (Amen).***

In English:

> **Blessed are You Lord our God, King of the universe, Who has sanctified us with His commandments and commanded us to kindle the festival lights. (Amen).**

Following this blessing, we add the *Shehecheyanu* as demonstrated previously:

Baruch ata Adonai, Eloheinu Melech ha-olam, shehecheyanu vekiyenamu, vehigianu la'zeman hazeh. (Amen).

In English:

Blessed are You Lord our God, King of the universe, Who gave us life, and sustains us, and enabled us to reach this season of joy. (Amen).

TABERNACLES (SUKKOT)

Live in booths for seven days: All native-born Israelites are to live in booths so your descendants will know that I had the Israelites live in booths when I brought them out of Egypt. I am the LORD your God.[112]

At the end of sundown on the last day of *Yom Kippur*, immediately plans begin for erecting the *sukkah*, or temporary dwelling associated with the holiday. What is a *sukkah*? A *sukkah* is a temporary dwelling with walls (made up of any material, but preferably something natural) and a roof made of a plant-material such as branches or bamboo. The regulations say that the stars should be visible through the gaps in the roof. At least three walls need to comprise the structure. It has to be at least four feet long, four feet wide and no more than thirty feet tall. It can resemble a tent or a hut made of branches. I have made them with a wooden frame covered in palm branches, but canvas walls are also used by others.

According to Steinburg's interpretation, the guidelines for creating a "kosher" and traditional *sukkah* are as follows:

---

[112] Leviticus 23:42-43

1. The *sukkah* must be built in an open space under the sky, so that it is not indoors or under dense foliage or the roof of any other structure.
2. As a temporary dwelling, it should be sturdy enough to sustain a normal wind, but just unstable enough so that it would not withstand a very strong gale.
3. The roof (*s'khakh*) must be made of plant material, such as cut branches, bamboo, or straw, but not grasses or leaves that dry quickly or have an unpleasant odor. Most people today use large palm fronds or reusable slatted palm mats.
4. The walls are less important than the *s'khakh* and can be made of any materials. There should be at least two-and-a-half walls, but most *sukkot* have at least three. The walls should also be no higher than 20 cubits (approximately 37 feet), no shorter than 10 handbreadths (approximately 36 inches), and have an area of at least 7 by 7 handbreadths, which is thought to be the necessary space for one person (approximately 26 inches squared).
5. The *s'khakh* must assume the principle of *tziltah merubah mechamatah*, which means the *sukkah* must be more shaded than sunlit. The s'khakh must be permeable enough for heavy rain to penetrate the *sukkah* and holey enough to reveal the stars to those inside the *sukkah* at night.
6. The walls must be fully built before the *s'khakh* is applied. Because the roof is the most significant aspect of the *sukkah*, we finish with that element. The walls may remain up from *Sukkot* to *Sukkot*, as long as the roof is newly applied (123).

These are the official guidelines; however, don't be discouraged if they sound complex. When actually building the *sukkah*, you might actually find that your creation is somewhat naturally inclined to follow the criterion above.

Decorating the *sukkah* can be exciting for children and adults alike. It allows all the fun and creativity of decorating a Christmas tree, but it is bigger and has greater decorative potential. Usually, very few other than the family cat, get to actually *sit* inside a decorated Christmas tree. The *sukkah*, with table and chairs inside, offers this unique benefit to the whole family. Often we use running lights, clear or colored, as well as harvest-themed ornaments. Traditionally, the children make paper chains as well as paper fruit and other crafts. Consider the weather. Some climates require decorators to make sure all creations are waterproof! For this, you can laminate the children's decorations or use a plastic substitute for paper. In hotter climates, sometimes artificial fruit containing wax or soft plastic has to be avoided due to the hot sun. The key here is to have fun in celebrating the bounty of the harvest—the richness of God's blessing. The cornucopia is most appropriate in a *sukkah*!

The *sukkah* is not just for decoration. There is a particular emphasis on eating in the *sukkah* on the first night of the holiday. We are encouraged to study, eat, talk and even sleep in our *sukkah*. If it is particularly uncomfortable, we are free to do fellowship and such elsewhere. We are also not expected to endure the rain while in the *sukkah*. This is not a holiday of afflicting ourselves, but one of enjoyment; this is a celebration of God's generous and bountiful gifts. The children find the *sukkah* to be such a fun opportunity to be "camping" and spending time outside in a different and fun environment with the whole family. Most adults also catch the excitement. This is definitely an engaging way to celebrate God—the sights, smells and excitement of the fruit decorations (such as cloves pressed into oranges) invoke such happy memories for those of us who have celebrated this previously. It has been said to incite new feelings of joy and anticipation akin to Christmas Eve for newcomers to the holiday.

Lighting the candles as described is customary on the first night (followed by the *shechechanu* for special occasions). In the context of blessings, the *sukkah* itself must be considered. The blessing for the *sukkah* is as follows:

Baruch ata Adonai, Eloheinu Melech ha-olam, asher kideshanu bemitzvotav vetzivanu leishev ba-sukkah. (Amen).

In English:

Blessed are You Lord our God, King of the universe, Who has sanctified us with His commandments and commanded us to live in the *sukkah*. (Amen).

This blessing is also recited after blessings for food, etcetera. Often, following the initial blessing for the *sukkah*, the *ushpizin*, or symbolic (my children call them "imaginary") guests, are invited to the *sukkah*. Each day, the guest is rotated. The traditional favorites are famous biblical "sojourners" who at some time in their life had to flee or wander. The popular ones are Abraham, Isaaac, Jacob, Joseph, Moses, Aaron, and David. Recent history has added Sarah, Rachel, Rebekah, Leah, Miriam, Abigail and Esther. Some Sephardic Jews set aside a decorated chair for the imaginary guest of the day. Also, we are encouraged to invite and host flesh-and-blood guests in our *sukkot* in the spirit of good will and celebration as our *tzedakah*, our contribution to charity.

FOUR SPECIES (ARBA MINIM)

On the first day you are to take choice fruit from the trees, and palm fronds, leafy branches and poplars, and rejoice before the LORD your God for seven days. Celebrate this as a festival to the LORD for seven days each year.[113]

Another integral part of *Sukkot* is the blessing and thanksgiving made with the *arba minim*. Literally "four species," the *arba minim* refers to a spray of different botanical branches and a citron. These are the

---

[113] Lev 23:40-41

four species as interpreted from the *Torah*: choice fruit (*etrog*, or citron), palm frond (*lulav*, or young date palm), leafy branches (*hasadim*, or myrtle), and poplars (*aravot*, or willows). Strassfeld comments, "These four species help emphasize the agricultural nature of *Sukkot*. Just as the farmer harvests his crops, so we gather four kinds of growing things and use them to praise God for the bounty He has provided us" (1985:129).

The *arba minim* are together both held and shaken while blessings to God are being recited. Usually the palm, myrtle and willow are held together with a woven sheath with only the *etrog* loose and thus held next to the *lulav* with the other hand. The procedure is as follows:

- Face East (or towards Jerusalem).
- Place the lulav (with all three branches) in the right hand with the spine towards you. (note: the spine is the long green ridge that runs the length of the young palm frond).
- Hold the *etrog* in your left hand with the *pitom* (or tip) pointing down (be careful not to damage it). Make sure the stem scar on the fruit is facing upwards.
- Recite the blessing as follows:

Baruch ata Adonai, Eloheinu Melech ha-olam, asher kideshanu bemitzvotav vetzivanu al netilat lulav. (Amen).

In English:

Blessed are You Lord our God, King of the universe, Who has sanctified us with His commandments and commanded us to wave the *lulav* [palm branch]. (Amen).

Once the blessing (and *Shehecheyanu* if the *sukkah* blessing was recited for the first time this year) is completed, the *etrog* is turned upside-up and and the *lulav* is shaken. The shaking of the *lulav* is also a very detailed part of the ritual, like most observances in Judiasm. With the *lulav* and *etrog* held as instructed previously, together they are shaken.

1. First, standing straight and erect and still facing Jerusalem, shake the *lulav* and *etrog* towards the East and then bring them back in front of you. Repeat this three times.
2. Second, shake towards the South and then bring the *arba minim* back in front of you. Repeat this three times.
3. Third, shake the *arba minim* over your shoulder (West). Replace it back in front of you and repeat this action three times.
4. Fourth, shake it to the North in the same manner. Do this three times. Each time be sure to bring it back in front of you.
5. Fifth, shake it towards the heavens. Do this three times likewise.
6. Finally, shake it towards the ground. Do this three times as before.

This covers all places where God is, as God is everywhere. This way, all directions are covered in waving the species towards God in thanks. After the holiday is done, it is also customary to chop up the *etrog* for use in the *havdalah* spice holder or to make marmalade out of it. The *lulav* is often dried and save to burn with the *chametz* (leavened products) before Passover.

The Ceremony lasted a week, with the last day being "*Hoshana Rabba*, meaning the day of the "Great *Hosanna*." People act here in a manner that we might recognize in conjunction to the Messiah's triumphant entry into Jerusalem. People would wave palm branches while singing and shouting, "*Hosanna*" which means literally, "save us."[114] During this week, however, the priests would be heavily involved—blowing *shofarot* (ram's horns) and waving palm branches themselves while the people sang what is referred to as the "*Great Hallal*" consisting of Psalms 113 through 118.

---

[114] Matthew 21:9, 21:15, Mark 11:9-10, John 12:13

During this time, the Temple was illuminated. Sons of the priests and young Levites would climb tall ladders to light high lamps all around the Temple and its court. Tradition tells of the light being seen from all around as it lit up the city for the week of celebration. This was the official illumination of the Temple and was part of the exciting festivities that the Jewish nation chose to use in celebrating this week-long "appointment" with their Creator. God was always with them, but this was the week to celebrate it with an extra measure of intimacy and heartfelt joy.

Along with the celebratory building of the tabernacles, shaking of the *lulav*, sounding of the *shofar* or illuminating of the Temple, the symbol of water was also of notable importance during this time of celebration. Leading up to the festival, the rabbis would teach and expound upon themes involving water. Of Older Testament times, it is written:

> Gold pitchers of water were brought from the pool of Siloam to the Temple. The priest would pour out water over the altar to signify Israel's gratitude for the rain that had produced the harvest, and would pray for rain in the next year. The priest would recite Isaiah 12:1-3, "And in that day thou shalt say, O LORD, I will praise Thee: though Thou wast angry with me, Thine anger is turned away, and Thou comfortedst me. Behold, God is my salvation; I will trust, and not be afraid: for the LORD …is my strength and my song; He also is become my salvation. Therefore with joy shall ye draw water out of the wells of salvation." This special libation was performed only during the …Feast of Tabernacles (Sampson, 1999:348).

This water ceremony was enacted for two reasons: 1., this would be a way of appealing to God for plentiful rains in the winter season as well as, 2. to keep the people focused on the coming Messiah who would be the source of these waters of salvation.

JESUS AND TABERNACLES (YESHUA IN SUKKOT)

Sukkot points to the Messiah in several ways. As mentioned above, the water libation ritual alluded to Yeshua. It was at this time that he turned to the people and taught them of the water of life. Scripture tells the story:

> *On the last and greatest day of the Feast, Jesus stood and said in a loud voice, "If anyone is thirsty, let him come to me and drink. Whoever believes in me, as the Scripture has said, streams of living water will flow from within him." By this he meant the Spirit, whom those who believed in him were later to receive. Up to that time the Spirit had not been given, since Jesus had not yet been glorified.*[115]

Here Yeshua is pointing directly to himself as the source of living water. On this "last and greatest day of the feast," Yeshua gives testimony to his own messiahship by this announcement. Yeshua is intrinsically tied into this theme of living water for *Sukkot* as well as closely associated with the theme of the Tabernacle; he himself was a means for God to dwell with humanity.

Yeshua is not only the Living Water, but also the Light of the World. The illuminated Temple during the Feast could not be hidden. The bright glow of its lamps lit up the city and is a fitting metaphor for our Savior who can illuminate the darkest corners of our lives, expelling the darkness of ignorance, guilt and shame forever. To him, we sing, "Hosanna" even now—"save us," knowing that he hears us now even as he did then. The many symbols of the holiday contribute to the sweetness of God dwelling with us as our champion who saves us, our Light who illuminates us, our Living Water who quenches us, and our intimate friend who dwells with us—all while maintaining omnipotent status.

---

[115] John 7:37-39

The imagery continues, as we look closer at Yeshua as a tabernacle himself. This points us once again to the time of the ancient Older Testament tabernacles with Israelites dwelling together in the desert as nomadic people. Their wandering was forever immortalized by the commemoration of it with this re-enactment of worshipping and dwelling in the temporary booths. It was during this time of wandering in the desert that the Tabernacle became a symbol of God enjoying fellowship with humanity. Scripture quotes God: "I will put my dwelling place among you, and I will not abhor you. I will walk among you and be your God, and you will be my people."[116] God dwelt among the people by using the Tabernacle here. Later, God dwelt with humanity in a different type of Tabernacle: "The Word became flesh and made his dwelling among us. We have seen his glory, the glory of the One and Only, who came from the Father, full of grace and truth.[117]

Fischer describes the apostle Peter at the Transfiguration. Seeing the glory of the Messiah, Peter thought of *Sukkot*:

> ... he immediately thought the Messiah had come to rule. In the spirit of the Zechariah passage [14:16-19], he appropriately suggested that they begin celebrating *Sukkot*. His idea was good, but his timing was off... [he] discovered later that he had had the privilege of looking into the future that Zechariah had predicted. So *Sukkot* pictures the coming reign of Messiah over the earth, that time of ultimate freedom (Fischer, 2004: accessed 04 Aug 2010).

If you wonder why Peter suddenly and seemingly out of context begins to offer to build them houses—he isn't. He is talking about making a Tabernacle, booth or *sukkah* in celebration of the fulfillment of the prophecy of *Sukkot*—God dwelling with humanity in the Messiah's reign over the earth.

---

[116] Leviticus 26:11-12
[117] John 1:14

When we celebrate the earthly, physical and temporal Tabernacle, in a deeper sense we also celebrate the concept of God dwelling with us, as He did through His son. Thus, the image of God dwelling with man also became apparent in God dwelling in flesh—that living Tabernacle dwelling with humankind in the form of Yeshua.

GOD WITH US

We can argue quite legitimately that the theme of this holiday is one of "Immanuel" meaning "God with us." From the very origin of the festival's theme—"tabernacling," or dwelling together in the wilderness, it was a very unique time in the history of humankind when God dwelled with humanity on earth in a way as never before. To further the Immanuel theme, the *sukkah* as described previously, had to have a very sparse roof so that, symbolically, there was no real barrier between God and man, between the Sovereign of Heaven and His children on earth. Even the *lulav* that is shaken in all directions, symbolizing God's presence everywhere, serves to emphasize the absolute honor and privilege of humanity that such an infinite God would choose to dwell with mortal humanity in such intimacy. It is saying that although God is everywhere, this week He chooses to be specifically here with us. For, while God is in all places, God is more importantly *with us* during this special Feast of Tabernacles—Immanuel.

To fully appreciate the meaning of God dwelling with humanity, we should analyze what it means to really "dwell." The meaning of the word in this context is not referring to someone simply living in proximity to another. I remember once while traveling back and forth to Scotland alone while I was studying at the University of St. Andrews, I would feel so alone and homesick even while in a crowded train station. Dwelling with someone in the connotation of the Feast of Tabernacles denotes an intimacy—a best friend, a spouse. God wants to dwell with us. He wants to know what is bothering us and keeping us awake at two o'clock in the morning. He wants to know our deepest dreams and thoughts. He wants to be with us in both in proximity and in relationship—not just during this week, but always. What a wonderful theme to celebrate and cherish! The Feast of Tabernacles is divinely ordained just for this exciting purpose—to celebrate this opportunity for intimacy with our God, our Redeemer and friend.

The scriptural theme for this holiday is the book of *Ecclesiastes* (also called *Kohelet* in the Jewish Bible). This is initially puzzling. It seems fitting, initially, that perhaps the other of Solomon's books would be more appropriate—Song of Solomon, a book of romantic love and a description of spouses dwelling together and confessing their love. In pessimistic contrast is the book that Solomon wrote later in life when he became disillusioned with the temporal world and writes of his own life's achievements "vanity, vanity, all is vanity."[118] How does this unromantic book fit with our theme of the Feast of Tabernacles, the idea of Immanuel—God dwelling with us? To unravel this mystery, we have to examine Ecclesiastes' theme by analyzing its most prominent words: "vanity," "man" (as in frail mortal) and "sun." These words are repeated most throughout the book to convey the message that *all man does under the sun is vanity*. This implies, then, that what really matters is what man does in the heavenly realm "over the sun." Thus the tie begins to materialize before us, as the only thing that counts is what we invest spiritually with God. When we invest time and effort for heavenly things with God, and we allow Him to dwell with us, the infinite God beyond the sun fills the whole of feeble man, this human form made of temporal dust and whose triumphs are summed up as "vanity." Ecclesiastes teaches us that the great Divine can live with and in this small and insignificant race called humanity. This points to a Messianic message for Christians and believing Jews alike, as the theme is the same familiar one: Immanuel.

---

[118] Ecclesiastes 2:2

HOW CAN THIS BENEFIT YOU, A CHRISTIAN?

Followers of Yeshua crave his presence, the outpouring of his living water and spirit. This holiday is a very appropriate time to remember these three things:

First, this is the day commemorating the walk with our Creator and dedicated to the celebration of not only God's blessings (as in harvest), but His dwelling with us as His people. God dwelled with the biblical forefathers in the wilderness in a tabernacle. God dwelled again with us through a baby, the Word of God made flesh. The theme of "Immanuel," usually only associated with Christmas, is a worthy theme and should be celebrated and fully enjoyed. Although God wants to dwell with us always, we can set aside time to focus and celebrate the joy of this privilege during this appointed time.

Second, this gives us an opportunity to meditate upon the Messianic Savior, the Light and Living Water from whom if one drinks, one shall never thirst again. The imagery and symbols are rich and filled with blessings and hidden lessons pointing to the Messiah. Yeshua refers to himself as a Temple,[119] a permanent replacement of the tabernacle dedicated to the joining together of the Divine with the human.

Third, as people of the twenty-first century, we celebrate all the trivial joys, accomplishments, and victories in life (all the "vanities" Solomon speaks of), so why not commemorate a most deserving holiday, a day dedicated to enjoying and celebrating our intimacy with God and our spiritual investments "over the sun?"

Even while we celebrate this great and rich Feast of Tabernacles for a week plus a day, building lovely tabernacles, being thankful to God for our blessings and the bounty God gives (rewarding traditions to be sure), we can do so much more. God wants us to commune with Him, to confide our deepest wishes and dreams to His awaiting ear. God wants to cry with us in our sorrows and to shout for joy with us in our victories. He

---

[119] John 2:19

wants to truly DWELL with us. Paul states that we are living tabernacles ourselves; we are each a *sukkah* of flesh, too.[120] Even while celebrating this feast, do more. While an eight-day long honeymoon would be great for couples once a year, how many marriages would survive if that eight days was the only time the couple spent together? What about the daily lives, the everyday comfort of just *being* together? That's also what God wants. Sure, celebrate togetherness during the Feast of Tabernacles—and enjoy it to the fullest, but don't stop there. Invite (or re-invite, if applicable) God to dwell with you in your heart's tabernacle—not just for a week, not for a week and a day, but for always

HOLIDAY NOSHES (SNACKS)

Since this is the time of the harvest, I have found so many recipes to be appropriate using this theme. One of our favorite harvest foods is pumpkin. This is a great addition to your *Sukkot* festival at home!

SUKKOT PUMPKIN BREAD (pareve)

Ingredients

- 3 eggs
- 1/2 cup oil
- 2 cups of brown sugar
- 1 teaspoon vanilla
- 2 cups of cooked pumpkin, mashed smoothly
- 1 teaspoon baking soda
- 1 1/2 teaspoons baking powder
- 3 teaspoons cinnamon
- 1/2 teaspoon allspice

---

[120] I Corinthians 6:19

- 1/2 teaspoon ginger
- 1/2 cup nuts (preferably walnuts)
- 3 cups flour

Variation

- 1/8 teaspoon of powdered cloves
- Icing: 1 1/2 cup powdered sugar with enough pineapple juice to make a glaze.

Directions

1. Preheat oven to 325 F
2. Mix together eggs, oil, sugar and vanilla for 1 minute (until smooth consistency).
3. Add pumpkin and mix with batter
4. Combine baking soda, baking powder, spices, nuts and flour
5. Mix dry ingredients well
6. Blend into batter mixture
7. Pour into two greased 9" x 3" x 3" loaf pans or equivalent
8. Bake at 325 degrees Fahrenheit until firm and golden brown, about 1 hour
9. Test for doneness by inserting a toothpick. (When it comes out clean, baking is done)
10. ENJOY!

CITRON (ETROG) CAKE (pareve)

Ingredients (cake)

- 1 citron (*etrog*)
- Juice of a lime

- 1 tablespoon of lemon juice
- 2 3/4 cups of flour
- 3 teaspoons baking powder
- 1/4 teaspoon salt
- 1/4 cup margarine
- 1 1/2 cups sugar
- 3 eggs
- 1 cup plus 1 tablespoon orange juice

Ingredients (glaze)

- 1 cup powdered sugar
- 1 teaspoon vanilla
- 1 tablespoon reserved citrus mixture
- 1 tablespoon orange juice

Variation

- Garnish with fresh mint leaves

Directions

1. Preheat oven to 375 degrees
2. Juice the citron and lime (strain out pulp and seeds)
3. Finely grate citron skin
4. Combine citron zest and citrus juices (including lemon) and set aside
5. Cream together margarine, sugar and eggs
6. Sift together flour, salt and baking powder

7. Combine all cake ingredients together, mixing well into a batter (saving aside at least 1 tablespoon of citrus juice mixture for glaze)
8. Spray non-stick spray into a tube pan
9. Bake 30-45 minutes or until toothpick inserted in the middle comes out clean
10. Remove cake from pan when partially cooled by tapping on the bottom
11. Combine remaining citrus mixture, powdered sugar, orange juice and vanilla.
12. Mix together well until glaze consistency (add more powdered sugar if glaze is too thin)
13. Drizzle over cooled cake
14. ENJOY!

REJOICING WITH GOD: CLIMAX OF HIGH HOLY DAYS THE EIGHTH DAY OF ASSEMBLY (SHEMINI ATSERET)

AND THE REJOICING OF THE FIVE BOOKS OF MOSES (SIMCHAT TORAH)

On the Jewish calendar: 22-23 *Tishrei* (September-October)

On the eighth day hold an assembly and do no regular work. Present an offering made by fire as an aroma pleasing to YHVH, a burnt offering of one bull, one ram and seven male lambs a year old, all without defect. With the bull, the ram and the lambs, prepare their grain offerings and drink offerings according to the number specified. Include one male goat as a sin offering.[121]

Literally interpreted as "The Assembly of the Eighth Day," *Shemini Atseret* is its own holiday. It lands on the eighth day after *Sukkot*. In Israel, it is

---

[121] Numbers 29:35-38

on the same day as *Simchat Torah*, the celebration of *Torah*, while in other places the days are two consecutive days.

Shemini Atseret, this eighth day holiday, is a climax in the communion between God and humanity that has transpired over the holidays preceding: *Rosh Hashanah*, *Yom Kippur* and especially *Sukkot*. God's holidays are divine appointments when we can fellowship with Him. *Sukkot*, being the holiday of God's dwelling with us, is a time of euphoric union with God. Like a romantic date with someone we desperately love, the end of it comes much too quickly. *Shemini Atseret* is best described thusly: God has enjoyed the company and fellowship of His people so much that He invites us to remain for an extra day.

This holiday occurs at the wintery part of the year. Although technically in autumn, it is more accurately classified as an early winter celebration. The harvest is over. Introspection, repentance and rejoicing have taken place. The wild celebrations of *Sukkot* are to be finalized with another period of introspection with *Shemini Atseret* followed by the euphoric gala of *Simchat Torah* in commemorating the reading of the last section of the *Torah* in Deuteronomy and beginning over again in Genesis.[122]

Shimini Atseret continues a theme of water. As *Sukkot* features water and water-pouring to show appreciation for the life-sustaining fluid, *Shimini Atseret* both continues and intensifies this theme—appealing to the Divine for rain. Since Passover, the nation has prayed for dew to keep the earth moist, as summer is not a time for rainfall. Now, the request changes; the prayer is for an abundance of rain (Waskow, 1982:70). The existence of a nation relied directly upon access to water. Water was vital for survival for both the Jews and their livestock. In pleading for water, they were beseeching the Divine for the very continuation of their existence—their very lives. The nation was blessed with life-giving water

---

[122] The *Torah* is divided into sections. During each week throughout the year, a section of the *Torah* is read in synagogues worldwide. *Simchat Torah* occurs when the last section is read, and the first one is begun all over again.

when attaining the approval of God and cursed with famine when transgressing. Here, the importance of water is revealed:

> *It shall come about, if you listen obediently to my commandments which I am commanding you today, to love the LORD your God and to serve Him with all your heart and all your soul, that He will give the rain for your land in its season, the early and late rain, that you may gather in your grain and your new wine and your oil. He will give grass in your fields for your cattle, and you will eat and be satisfied. Beware that your hearts are not deceived and that you do not turn away and serve other gods and worship them, or the anger of the LORD will be kindled against you, and He will shut up the heavens so that there will be no rain and the ground will not yield its fruit; and you will perish quickly from the good land which the LORD is giving you.*[123]

Israel's survival was directly related to her abundance of water for human consumption, livestock and vegetation. Without it, the people were destined for both failure and misery and quite often death.

THE HIGH HOLIDAYS AND SHEMINI ATSERET IN SONG OF SOLOMON

The day of *Shimini Atseret* and the High Holidays (*Rosh Hashanah*, The Days of Awe, *Yom Kippur*, & *Sukkot*) are best described in relation to this featured verse in *Song of Solomon* because of their theme of repentance, reconciliation and love. Simcha Benyosef makes the connection between the famous romantic prose and the High Holidays (1999:136-137). The song reads:

> *I am sleeping, but my heart is awake*
> *A sound! My Beloved knocks!*

---

[123] Deuteronomy 11:13-17 NASB

Open to Me, my sister, my love,
My dove, My perfect one.[124]

Shemini Atseret represents the climax of togetherness with God as it is the culmination of the solemnity and soul-seeking that began before *Rosh Hashanah* and the days of repentance. The above verse in *Songs of Solomon* maps out the progression of the relationship between humanity and the Divine.

In analyzing the verse alongside the holiday calendar, we come to our first parallel. Notice first is the statement, "I am sleeping, but my heart is awake." During the year building up to the fall holidays of repentance, one can be considered to be outwardly sleeping but inwardly awake. During the duration of the year, we serve God and endeavor to live righteously, however we are not collectively soul-searching and repenting as we are during the holidays of repentance beginning with *Rosh Hashanah*. We are "asleep"—but we are not unconscious, for our heart is awake. We live in anticipation.

In the stillness of this time, a sound is heard. "A sound! My Beloved knocks!" says *Song of Solomon*. As we journey through the year, we come to *Rosh Hashanah*, a God-appointed time to stop, look and listen. We hear the very knock of God upon our hearts—hearts that have been vigilant despite our inanimate period of silence—the inactivity of the summer months devoid of holidays.[125] Sleeping or not, if our hearts are not listening, we will not hear the sound, the knock. The awful sound of *Rosh Hashanah's shofar*, the call to wake up to repentance accompanies this rousing Divine knock. Awake, awake! The theme is one of being startled out of our humdrum everyday complacence. We are brought to our knees in something akin to fear and trembling—we examine ourselves and repent sincerely. We grieve our sins and confess them. We mend our ways and make resolutions to begin anew with God. We are in our

---
[124] Songs of Solomon 5:2
[125] These are the holidays other than the weekly *Shabbat* or monthly *Rosh Chodesh*.

proverbial sackcloth and ashes, mending the wrongs and transgressions of our past and present. We leave no stone unturned. We are startled into action. We are motivated to leave the past wrongs, going forth with a new start—a new and closer walk with the Divine.

This brings us to the onset of *Yom Kippur*. We are no longer in a startled state. We have repented and are now seeking His face. We have no more fear of accusers, as they have no sway upon us, for we are clean. We are cleansed and lifted from our ashes. His love for us begins to shine brighter as our souls are reconfirmed as companions to His own. We are now able to open to His knock, to answer His call and to return His embrace. The next line of the verse reflects just this, "Open to Me, my sister, my love." We are now to find the face of our Divine Love. We are His, we are of Him and can be called His Love.

After this initial love, we progress to a deeper form of love. We are not in the "new love" but rather "true love" phase. Our love begins to transform into a raw and insatiable passion for God and His precepts. We are not motivated by fear or even by a comfortable love but by a consuming motivation that dramatically alters our experience. We are now in the arms of God. We are becoming one with Him. A beautiful and intimate bonding takes place—our soul uniting with God's. We are his Love and His own, and He calls us, in endearment, "My dove."

United with God, we are now enjoying the euphoria of this spiritual oneness. We feel God so close that He is actually within. We can rejoice and celebrate the mutual union—God is not only surrounding us, He is within us and we in Him. This is indescribable, and the final stage of our relationship with God. This is a taste of Heaven. This total and ineffable unity with God is equally joyous for the Divine as He turns to us and proclaims in the height of His love and pleasure, "My perfect one." Our blemishes are lost to both God and ourselves. We cannot be imperfect while enjoined to the epitome of perfection. His righteousness covers us, rendering us perfectly accepted, perfectly His and perfect in Him.

TRADITIONAL OBSERVANCE

Shemini Aseret and *Simchat Torah* are celebrated with a blessing of the *Shechecheyanu*. After the blessing and often some liturgy, the congregation's attention is turned to singing and dancing. I thoroughly enjoy the Jewish holidays throughout the year; however the most exciting holiday experience I have ever had, however, and trumping all of these is the thrill of *Simchat Torah*.

The tradition of *Simchat Torah* celebration includes a mandatory dance with the *Torah* encircling the reading table in the synagogue (or entire room in some congregations) at least seven times while singing. Some congregations play music and sing until everyone has had at least one dance with the *Torah*. The one holding the *Torah* leads the procession until handing it off to the next participant. Children follow with miniature *Torah* scrolls and colorful flags, singing and rejoicing over the word of God. I remember the first time I held the *Torah*. It was warm from the other dancers before me. Its soft velvet cover caressed my cheek while the silver crowning ornaments tinkled and clanked above. The *yod*, hanging on its chain, swung in rhythm as I led the procession. The precious weight in my hands was the word of God, the closest I could come to dancing with the Word of God in the flesh. I remember the smiles and dancing around me fading away as I closed my eyes and enjoyed this moment, this dance with the word of God. It was one of the sweetest feelings that I cannot describe. Dancing with this parchment version of the Word foreshadows that dance for joy we shall share one unspeakable day when we dance with the Word in the flesh.

HOW CAN THIS BENEFIT YOU, A CHRISTIAN?

Our relationship with God can be mapped out on the Jewish calendar, especially during the High Holidays. Four distinct stages of our relationship with God are illustrated beautifully. Experiencing these days in sequence and in the intended spirit of each of the holidays brings a model of a personal relationship with God. As Israel was given a corporate experience; we are also given the opportunity for a personal one. God and I can be together as one.

1. **Awe.** As demonstrated in the verse of *Song of Solomon*, we come to God in steps. Our relationship may begin as one that is strained, estranged or distant. The first step we make in our progress towards God is to recognize Him and His power. This brings us to the phase of Awe. This can also be understood as intense respect to the point of outright fear. When we see the greatness of God and the comparative smallness of ourselves, we are humbled and overwhelmed. Upon trying to fathom the grandness of God, we must come to a realization of Who exactly He is. He is terrible and great, fearsome and majestic. All of our worldly importance becomes nothing in His proximity. We must either acknowledge His greatness and succumb to it or reject Him altogether to our own ruin. We see our shortcomings and our need for a Savior—we see how we fall short of the Divine standard and seek the forgiveness of God and the atoning blood of Yeshua. Once we humble ourselves and repent, we take on the spirit of *Rosh Hashanah* in our lives. We are beginning a relationship with God and allow the awe of His greatness to inspire us into new beginnings and straighter paths. We are covered by the blood of the Passover Lamb, the sacrifice of Yeshua, and begin to yearn for and partake of salvation.

2. **Love.** When we give ourselves to God and surrender our lives over to His will, we become first-hand witnesses to His greatness and endless love. We appreciate the sacrifice of Yeshua, and his death becomes more real to us as we simultaneously feel our unworthiness combined with intense gratitude for his grace. We see our own unworthiness in light of His goodness and become

overwhelmed by His blessings and forgiveness. When we make changes and sacrifices in our lives for God, we constantly find that the blessings far outweigh them. We realize that we cannot possibly out-trust, out-give or out-love God. The result is that we love Him back—loving Him because He so deeply first loved us.

3. **Passion.** In our relationship with God, when we allow ourselves to see and partake of God's love and benevolence, we fall more and more in love—allowing Him to flow through us. This brings us to a passionate relationship with our God. Yeshua lives in us. We begin to truly "know" Him—as in an intimate closeness singularly found in the marriage model. We are the bride of the Messiah Yeshua and eagerly embrace him into every aspect of our lives. Like an obsessed young bride, we each are consumed and completely preoccupied with our Messiah. He is in our every waking thought; the sheer thought of Him brings a smile to our face and warmth to our soul. We are passionately in love with Yeshua, our Bridegroom.

4. **Union.** Our passion and fervor for our Savior continues as an all-consuming pre-occupation. His holy flame becomes one with ours. We are one in him and united in his purpose and character. We reveal him to those around us, as he is in us and in each aspect of our lives. We are still human but are covered by the glory of God so that we are one with him. We, as the body and bride of Yeshua, are wed and living as One and producing fruit by living our love and thereby winning more souls to the Kingdom.

FEAST OF DEDICATION or FESTIVAL OF LIGHTS[126] (CHANUKAH)

On the Jewish calendar: 25 *Kislev* (Nov-Dec)

At that time the Feast of Dedication took place at Jerusalem; it was winter, and [Yeshua] was walking in the temple in the portico of Solomon.[127]

HOLIDAY BACKGROUND

Chanukah (commonly spelled *Hanukkah*) is one of the most well-known of the Jewish holidays due to its proximity to Christmas. It is not a major holiday and only makes a small cameo appearance in the Christian Newer Testament. Some think it is the Jewish substitute for Christmas. Assimilated Jews are known to bring "*Chanukah* bushes" (*Chanukah*-themed "Christmas trees") into the house to decorate. Traditionally speaking, the gift-giving and elaborate decorations of many *Chanukah* celebrations rival those of Christmas and are not genuinely part of *Chanukah*. In an

---

[126] This is not to be confused with other completely unrelated religious festivals and celebrations of light such as *Chaharshanbe Suri* (part of the Persian New Year celebration dating back to the early Zoroastrian era) or *Diwali* (a religious festival associated with Hinduism, Sikhism and Jainism).
[127] John 10:22-23 NASB

odd twist of irony, the very day that celebrates miracles and the Jewish refusal to assimilate has become what might be considered the most secular and assimilated Jewish holiday today.

THE STORY

With a recurring theme of religious freedom and national survival, the ancient *Chanukah* story echoes triumph and ultimate victory in the face of great odds—with the help of a few miracles. This takes us back to the second century B.C.E. during the inter-testament period (between the Older and Newer Testaments). The story is related in the apocryphal books of *I and II Maccabees*. During this time, the Greeks were expanding their ever-increasing empire with goals of spreading their culture throughout the world—having already been successful in much of the Middle East and Asia. Thus, Judea, Egypt and Syria were all conquered by Alexander the Great and Hellenized accordingly. Alexander did allow the conquered nations to worship according to their own wishes. Consequently, so many Jews, without feeling a direct threat to their identity, became complacent about retaining their own Jewishness. Many began to adopt a Hellenist way of dressing, speaking and conducting the business of daily life. They assimilated into Greek society.

Antiochus IV, a much more intolerant monarch, came to power during the second century B.C.E. His policies were not as relaxed. He banned the practice of Judaism, killed many of the resisting Jews and placed a Hellenized priest in the Temple. During this time, the Temple became desecrated. Pigs were sacrificed upon the Temple altar—a great insult of great defilement against the God of Israel. This could not be tolerated by the religious sects of Jews that remained. They had to stop this sacrilege!

The revolt was organized secretly and carried out swiftly. The resistance was small in number, but great in spirit. They were passionate about reclaiming and cleansing the Temple to make it once again worthy of God's presence. Mattathias the Hasmonean and Judah Maccabee (his son) led out the rebellion.[128] They fought valiantly against both Hellenism itself and the assimilation of their fellows into the Greek culture. They fought together tenaciously against the Seleucid Greek state. Although the grassroots Maccabean army was ridiculously outnumbered by hoards of trained Greek warriors, they were nonetheless victorious. This was a miracle. The Temple was now free for the cleansing.

Aside from unclean sacrificial practices, many things had contributed to the defilement of the holy Temple of God. Idols, pagan offerings and tools of worship littered the sacred space. With the battle won and behind them, the Maccabees and their supporters honed their focus in on the cleansing and rededication of the Temple.

Once ready for rededication, however, only one day's worth of oil was available for the Temple *menorah* (candelabra). It would take eight days to procure a fresh supply of oil. The single day's ration of oil was nevertheless put into the menorah and lit. The oil remained alight for the eight days until the new supply was brought in. This was the second miracle. Thus, this time of victory and miracles marks our calendars as *Chanukah*, or "Dedication."

TRADITIONAL OBSERVANCE

Chanukah, one of the minor holidays (like *Purim*) is one of my children's favorites (also like *Purim*). The lights, singing, spirit of victory, *dreidel* games and holiday foods all contribute to its glowing reputation to the youngest in our home. Aside from the fun, singing and parties (perhaps we are guilty of some degree of "*Chanukah* assimilation" as well), we draw our attention to God's miracles--the highlight of the holiday. The themes this season are miracles and light—and we aim to give both topics their due in our celebrations.

---

[128] Members of what was to be known later as Pharisaism were also to join the revolt.

CANDLES

We begin the day with blessings and candles. On the first day of *Chanukah*, two candles are used--the *shamash* helper candle (usually in the center, at a different height, and/or otherwise differentiated from the main eight candles) and a candle representing the first day of *Chanukah*. Notice the *menorah* for this holiday, a *Chanukiah* (or *Hanukkiah*) holds nine candles total. This may be confusing, as the normal Temple-type *menorah* holds only seven. This *menorah* holding nine candles is special, as it is uniquely fashioned for *Chanukah*. This way, aside from the *shamash* candle, eight candles are ultimately lit, representing miracle of the eight days of oil.

The *shamash* candle is lit first. A *shamash* candle will be used each night of *Chanukah* to light the other candles before finding its own place in its holder. Once the *shamash* is lit, the candle representing the first day of *Chanukah* can be lit with it. What is the purpose of a *shamash* candle that is not considered one of the *Chanukah* candles? The *Chanukah* candles are to be enjoyed only. They are not to serve any other purpose--not light to read by and not fire to begin other fires. Therefore, a *Chanukah* candle cannot be used to light another candle, as it thereby becomes a tool. To alleviate this dilemma, another candle is given this task to be such a tool as a servant candle to the others, the *shamash*.

The *Chanukiah* must have one *Chanukah* candle added per day. In a traditional *Chanukiah* that resembles the Temple menorah in style (with four curved branches and candle holders on each side and a candle holder in the middle), a single candle is added the first night beginning on the right-hand side. On the first night, therefore, you would have a candle on the far right branch and a *shamash* candle with which to light it in the middle candle holder. On the second night, two candles would be placed into the two far right-hand candle holders. On the third night, three on the three far right-hand holders and so forth, working across the *Chanukiah* one night and one candle at a time—each time with the *shamash* faithfully burning in its holder of different height or otherwise separate from the configuration. However, although we add candles from the right to left in the direction the Hebrew language reads, we actually light the candles from the left to the right in celebration of the candle as a symbol of this "new" day that has not been commemorated yet in the season.

This, like all candle-lighting, is done with ceremony and blessings for the holiday. For this particular holiday, however, candle lighting is one of the main observances. While holding the *shamash* and lighting the first candle, this blessing is spoken or sung as follows:

> *Baruch ata Adonai, Eloheinu Melech ha-olam, asher kideshanu bemitzvotav vetzivanu lehadlik ner shel Chanukah. (Amen).*

In English:

> **Blessed are You Lord our God, King of the universe, Who has sanctified us with His commandments and commanded us to kindle the lights of *Chanukah*. (Amen).**

The next blessing is added:

> *Baruch ata Adonai, Eloheinu Melech ha-olam shehasah nissim lavoteynu beyamim ha-heym bazman hazeh. (Amen).*

In English:

> **Blessed are You, Lord our God, King of the universe, who worked miracles for our forebears in those days at this very season. (Amen).**

As occurs on most holidays, these are followed by the *Shechecheyanu*, the blessing for the new season (as previously demonstrated). Often, the following is also sung or recited:

We kindle these lights on account of the miracles, the wonders, the liberations, and the battles that You carried out for our forebears in these days at this time of year, through the hands of Your holy priests. For all eight days of Chanukah these lights are holy. We are not allowed to used them; they are only to look at, in order to thank and praise Your great name on account of Your miracles, Your wonders, and Your liberations (Waskow, 1982:95).

When the blessings are done, our family reflects together upon God's miracles in our lives and our answered prayers. We each recall a time we knew God was with us or answered our prayers. We do this each night. We gaze into the candle light and pause to reflect upon our own Savior--the Light of the world. After this, the family sings or has *Chanukah* music playing. Some of the most common songs are listed below.

SONGS [129]

ROCK OF AGES (MA'OZ TZUR)
(Hebrew [written approximately 1200 C.E.] and English)

Ma-oz tur yeshuati
Lecha na-eh leshabayah
Tikon Bety tefilati
Vesham todah nezabei-ach
Az egmor beshir mizmor
Chanukat ha-mizbei-ach

Rock of Ages, let our song,
Praise Thy saving power
Thou amidst the raging foes,
Was our sheltering tower

---

[129] Tunes can be found online by searching song title.

Furious they assailed us,
But Thine arm availed us
And Thy word broke their sword,
When our own strength failed us.
And Thy word broke their sword,
When our own strength failed us.

OH *CHANUKAH*, OH *CHANUKAH*[130]
(Yiddish and English)

Chanukah, Oh *Chanukah*
A yontev a sheyner
A lustiger a freylicher
Nito noch azoyner
Ale nacht in dreydl shpiln mir
Zudigheyse latkes esn mir

Geshvinder tsindt kinder
Di dininke lichtelech on
Zogt "al ha-nisim," loybt G-t far di nisim
Un kumt gicher tantsn in kon

Chanukah, Oh *Chanukah*
Come light the menorah
Let's have a party
We'll all dance the hora
Gather round the table, we'll have a treat
Shiny tops to play with, latkes to eat

And while we are playing
The candles are burning low
One for each night, they shed a sweet light
To remind us of days long ago

---

[130] Sometimes it is titled "Oh *Hanukkah,* Oh *Hanukkah.*"

DREIDEL GAME

Driedels are a big part of the fun and games part of *Chanukah*. What are *dreidels*? They resemble spinning tops with four flat sides. Basically, if you imagine dice with handles protruding from their tops and points for spinning on their bottoms, you can get the basic visualization of what a *dreidel* looks like. On each of the four sides is a Hebrew letter. These are נ (*Nun*), ג (*Gimmel*), ה (*Hay*) and ש (*Shin*). They are each part of an acronym "*Nes Gadol Hayah Sham*" which translates to English "A Miracle Happened There."[131] This is in reference to the oil miracle. In Yiddish, these letters also stand for the rules of the game, depending upon what letter is facing upwards after the *dreidel* is twirled and subsequently falls after its spin. Chocolate money is "gambled," in a pool in the center of the game. Each player adds a coin to the center pile and then spins a *dreidel* to determine their share of the booty. They take the following portions according to what letter the *dreidel* lands on. The spin result with determine the action taken. The symbols are interpreted as follows:

נ =*nit* (nothing), ג =*gantz* ([take] all), ה =*halb* ([take] half), and ש =*shtel* (put [in]). When the pot is empty, everyone puts a coin in again, and the game starts over. Fun!

HOW CAN THIS BENEFIT YOU, A CHRISTIAN?

The themes of *Chanukah* can be valued by Christians everywhere, themes of miracles, victory over persecution, triumph of Godly over ungodly and even basically, light illuminating darkness. Christian songs such as "This Little Light of Mine" are old classic spirituals that are tributes to this very Light. Our Savior is our Light. What better theme to such a bright and triumphant time? Yeshua is in this day symbolized by the light flooding darkness.

---

[131] In Israel, the four letters used are נ (*Nun*), ג (*Gimmel*), ה (Hay) and פ (*Pey*) for "*Nes Gadol Hayeh Po*," translated to "A Miracle Happened *Here*."

Miracles are also a great part of this time. In this post-modern society that we live in, supernatural phenomena are often scoffed at and considered to most to be on par with fairy tales. With popular science and commonly accepted beliefs denying the metaphysical world, if it cannot be proven in a laboratory, it simply does not exist. By such prevailing philosophy, miracles have been judged. Christians can benefit immensely by taking a time out of the year to sit with family and friends and recall the power of miracles and prayer. This is not only inspiring, but encouraging and spiritually invigorating. I highly recommend this practice, regardless of your commitment level in regards to Jewish (or biblical) holiday observance.

JESUS IN THE FEAST OF DEDICATION (YESHUA IN CHANUKAH)

Yeshua went to the Temple and celebrated this minor holiday at the Temple. The *Gospel of John* mentions this time of year and indicates that Yeshua is at the Temple as would be expected of an observant orthodox Jew, "At that time the Feast of Dedication took place at Jerusalem; it was winter, and Jesus was walking in the Temple in the portico of Solomon."[132] With this account present in the Newer Testament, perhaps we can assume that he observed the holiday according to the manner of his culture. He would have, therefore, said blessings and pondered the miracles surrounding the Maccabean story, celebrating the triumph of this passionate minority as well as the Temple oil's eight-day replenishment by unseen hands. The Messiah, as the Light of the World, is undoubtedly the most prominent part of the holiday in believing households—and was likely to have been so among those of the as well.

Yeshua referred to himself as the Temple.[133] In celebration the rededication of the Temple, we may also consider the significance of our own Savior, that Temple who took our sin upon himself to thus be "defiled" for our sakes. He was raised in three days in accordance to his prophecy

---

[132] John 10:22-23 NASB
[133] John 2:19

symbolized by the Temple imagery. He is yet our Temple, our method of meeting with God even now.

Likewise, we are also Temples in a lesser sense. Our bodies are Temples of the *Ruach HaKodesh* (Holy Spirit). Even though *Chanukah* occurs shortly after the High Holidays, *Chanukah* still provides an excellent opportunity to ensure that our own Temple is cleansed and in a state of dedication to our God. We can ask ourselves what defiles our Temple? What do we have inside us that does not belong? What needs to be cast out? God cannot dwell in an impure Temple, thus we must also likewise do another introspective examination and ensure that we are clean and welcoming to the indwelling of the Holy Spirit of God.

HOLIDAY NOSHES (SNACKS)

However unfortunate this may be for all health-wise fellows with low-fat diets, *Chanukah* is a time for consuming oily food. *Chanukah*'s eight days celebrate oil; therefore, most everything truly *Chanukah* is fried in it. If we only splurge once a year, however, the consequences are not too horrible. (This is what I tell myself anyhow). The most traditional *Chanukah* food is potato pancakes, or latkes. They are an excellent improvement to hash browns and are garnished with either apple sauce or sour cream. My kids like to eat them with ketchup, a very American touch to be sure.

CHANUKAH LATKES (pareve)

Ingredients

- 5 medium potatoes, grated
- 1 medium onion, grated
- 1/8 c. all purpose flour
- 1 egg
- 1 tsp. salt (or to taste)
- Vegetable oil

Variation

- Add grated or finely chopped veggies (carrots, parsley, celery, red peppers)
- Southwest version: green chilies and cheddar cheese (recipe becomes dairy)
- 1 whole egg can be replaced with 2 egg whites
- Low-fat: Patties can be baked in on greased cookie sheet at 450 until brown on top, turning over once. This saves lots of "fat calories" (but we can't do much about reducing the carbohydrates!)

Directions

1. Heat 1/8 inch of oil in pan
2. Combine grated potatoes and onion, draining juice if any
3. Lightly beat eggs
4. Mix salt and flour together
5. Mix flour and salt mixture with eggs until smooth
6. Combine egg flour mixture with potato/onion mixture
7. Test oil for heat (a piece of grated potato should sizzle)
8. Form palm-sized patties
9. Lower gently into hot oil
10. Fry both sides until golden brown
11. Drain well on paper towels
12. Serve with applesauce or sour cream (dairy).
13. ENJOY!

ISRAELI JELLY DOUGHNUTS (SUFGANIOT) (pareve)

These are more of an Israeli tradition as the name suggests, but they taste so good that we decided to adopt them into our celebration as well.

Ingredients

- 1 .25 oz. package rapid rise yeast
- 4 tablespoon sugar, divided
- 1 1/4 cup warm water, divided
- 3 1/2 cup all purpose flour, divided
- 1/4 cup margarine
- 1 egg plus 1 extra yolk
- Grated zest of an orange
- Vegetable oil for deep frying (2 inches in heavy pot)
- 1/2 cup seedless jam
- Powdered sugar to roll doughnut in

Variation

- Add some cinnamon to powdered sugar and use apple pie filling in lieu of jam

Directions

1. Dissolve the yeast and 1 tablespoon sugar into warm water. Let sit 10 min.
2. Combine frothy yeast mixture to flour (minus 1 tablespoon), egg plus yolk, salt, zest and remaining sugar.
3. Add margarine and work into sticky dough.
4. Transfer to a greased bowl, cover and let rise in warm place at least 1 hour

5. Add remaining flour (adding more if necessary) to make stiff dough.
6. Roll out dough to 1/2 inch thickness
7. Cut into circles approximately 2 inches in diameter (biscuit cutter), let rise 30 min.
8. Heat 2 inches of oil in heavy pot (375 F).
9. Lower doughnuts gently into hot oil allowing gaps between them.
10. Fry both sides 1-3 minutes until golden brown.
11. Drain well on paper towels.
12. Make slit in a side of the doughnut. Squeeze jam into center of doughnut with pastry bag (or turkey baster or even plastic bag with tiny part of corner tip cut off).
13. Roll or dust in powdered sugar and serve IMMEDIATELY.
14. ENJOY

BIRTHDAY OF TREES (TU B'SHEVAT)

On Jewish calendar: 15 *Shevat*

When you enter the land and plant any kind of fruit tree, regard its fruit as forbidden. For three years you are to consider it forbidden; it must not be eaten.[134]

Also known the "new year" holiday for trees, this dates back to Talmudic times, although the marking of a trees birthday, or date of planting, goes back to the time of Moses as indicated in the text above in counting the first three fruiting years. It is the also Jewish "Arbor Day," to use American language, yet it is more. While the Temple stood in the midst of Israel, the people all paid tax to support the priesthood. This was a tithing, a one-tenth tax on a citizen's increase. This increase was an equivalent to what we would call today "income." Waskow explains,

> The tithing system included a one-tenth tax on fruit. The tithe of fruit could only be given on behalf of the fruit crop of a given year out of the fruit that actually ripened that year. So in order to organize the tithe correctly there had to be a tax year—and agreed date by which to define the end of the fruit

---

[134] Leviticus 19:23

crop of the previous year, and the beginning of the fruit crop of the next year (1982:105-106)

Thus, this date, the fifteenth day of the month of *Shevat* became the fiscal year of a tree's taxation. Most of the winter rains had fallen by this point, the trees were soaking it up, and their sap was beginning to rise.

For centuries, this holiday was one of great celebration as a midwinter minor holiday. Always occurring during a full moon, it was a time of dances, festivals, weddings and betrothals. This bright night or night of light provided a fun time for evening activity—and celebrating the time of trees was always a perfect excuse to kick up one's heels. Adding to the holiday's gaiety was its marking of the transition from the severity of winter into a period of new life.

Trees themselves are an important symbol in the Bible. Immediately in Genesis, trees of both "Life" and "Good and Evil" are presented. The word of God is often described also as a "Tree of Life." God valued trees and later tells Moses that when Israel makes war against a land, the trees must be protected.[135] The Psalmist uses trees as imagery as well and describes the righteous man as one "planted by the water."[136] The cedars of Lebanon are mentioned throughout scripture in a very positive sense. Trees are prominent in scripture. Celebrating them, therefore, seems quite logical.

TRADITIONAL OBSERVANCE

The holiday, as previously mentioned, has been known in ancient times as a time for fun celebration with parties and dances. Today's observance is usually a little more subdued. Part of today's traditions involves eating fruit—an appropriate thing to do on this day marking the fiscal year of (fruiting) trees.

---

[135] Deuteronomy 20:19
[136] Psalm 1:3

Donating to charity is appropriate (as it is on all holidays). It is customary to donate *ninety-one* of a monetary denomination as a contribution to charity—cents, dollars, etc. This is because the value of ninety-one is the equivalent of the numerical value of the Hebrew letters that make up the word *ilan*, or tree.

Some households have a *Tu B'Shevat Seder*. This is a custom stemming from Sephardic and Israeli cultures. Four cups of wine symbolize the four seasons. These are blessed with the *Hagafen* blessing and drunk in sequence along with fruit and nuts sampled from three categories:

1. **The first category** is of fruits or nuts that have an *inedible shell or peel* (pistachio, avocado or pomegranate).
2. **The second category** holds fruits that can be *consumed wholly except for a pit* (apricot, date or olive).
3. **The third category** comprises fruit and nuts that can be *eaten whole* (berries, grapes, and figs).

The seder for *Tu B'Shevat* is not standardized, as many different communities are finding their own ways of celebrating and developing ways of expressing their appreciation for trees or fruit trees specifically. Experiment and create a *seder* that is right for your family. You can use fruit that is grown in the Holy Land or even fruit that is indigenous to your local area. The idea is to celebrate the joy of the trees and the fruit God has given us while instilling such an appreciation in our children.

Most obviously is the very appropriate "arbor day" custom of actually planting a tree (preferably a fruit tree)! If one cannot plant a tree in their yard, a donation can be made for planting one in Israel or as a memorial for a deceased loved one elsewhere. In Israel, planting trees to honor people is a very common custom. Even Gentiles who were heroic and "righteous" in aiding the Jewish people during World War II are honored with trees planted in their names. As for our family, we annually decorate the house with various "tree-themed" decorations such as artificial palm trees and lights for the children to enjoy. After all, this may be a minor holiday, but it is still a great opportunity to celebrate.

HOLIDAY NOSHES (SNACKS)

Eating fruity and nutty (particularly Holy Land type) foods during this time adds to the "tree" theme of the day. Some fun and popular *Tu B'Shevat* snacks include things with dates and nuts. Here is one of our favorites that the kids help out with.

STUFFED DATES AND FIGS (pareve)

Ingredients

- Half a dozen or so dried figs
- A dozen or so dates
- 2 cups almonds, walnuts and/or pecans
- 1/4 cup grated coconut

Directions

1. Cut figs and dates in half length-wise
2. Put a nut or nuts into each dried half
3. Roll in shredded coconut, squeezing the coconut onto the fruit
4. ENJOY!

FEAST OF LOTS (PURIM)

On Jewish calendar: 14-15 *Adar* [*Adar* II in leap years] (February-March)

Mordecai recorded these events, and he sent letters to all the Jews throughout the provinces of King Xerxes, near and far, to have them celebrate annually the fourteenth and fifteenth days of the month of Adar as the time when the Jews got relief from their enemies, and as the month when their sorrow was turned into joy and their mourning into a day of celebration. He wrote them to observe the days as days of feasting and joy and giving presents of food to one another and gifts to the poor.

So the Jews agreed to continue the celebration they had begun, doing what Mordecai had written to them. ... These days should be remembered and observed in every generation by every family, and in every province and in every city. And these days of Purim should never cease to be celebrated by the Jews, nor should the memory of them die out among their descendants.[137]

---

[137] Esther 9:20-23, 28

HISTORICAL BACKGROUND

The originating story of Queen Esther and her cousin Mordecai—the narration that prompted this holiday of *Purim*, occurred during the reign of King Ahasuerus (Xerxes) approximately around 486-465 B.C.E. Israel was living in the diaspora—Shushan (Persia) to be exact. Following the narration of the biblical Book of Esther, the *Purim* story follows the young Jewish orphan girl, Hadassah, and her guardian Mordecai.

THE STORY

Persian King Ahasuerus (Xerxes) holds a party, at which the decision is made that his queen, the stunningly attractive Vashti, make her appearance to show off one of the king's treasures—her own flesh, a body of unparalleled beauty. She would have most likely been requested to dance in the nude and exhibited in a manner that was quite humiliating, even for a woman well-entrenched in this male-dominated culture. Probably mortified at the prospect of parading as a communal plaything, she outright defies the king's invitation to the party and simply refuses to appear. This angers the reveling party, comprised of drunken partying men. Angered and disappointed that their "show" was cancelled, they collectively insist that the king both dethrone and banish her as an example to woman everywhere—that disobedience to men (husbands) will neither be tolerated nor met with impunity throughout the kingdom. The queen is then banished and disposed of altogether, leaving both king and kingdom queen-less.

The empty female throne must be filled, so the king announces a type of beauty pageant which promises that the winner will be crowned queen. All the virgins are gathered, forcibly, to the king's harem for a period of beautification that precedes their presentation to the king. Orphaned Hadassah finds herself among the young virginal contestants in this bizarre competition. She is instructed by her guardian and cousin, Mordecai, to hide her Jewish heritage. Therefore, she goes by the Persian name that we commonly know her by today, "Esther." Once the king spends time with Esther, he realizes that she is "the one." She is crowned as queen, and no one at court seems to know of her Jewish origins.

All seems to be going well in the kingdom until one of the king's closest men (think Prime Minister) begins to make trouble in the kingdom by plotting against the Jewish inhabitants of the land. This is the notorious Haman, descendant of the vanquished Israelite arch-enemy, the Amalekites.[138] Queen Esther's cousin, Mordecai, a faithful monotheist, refuses to bow to any earthly image or man. Haman's pride is irritated by this fact, as all are required to bow to him. Mordecai's refusal to bow to Haman becomes a primary catalyst in the story. Spurred by an insatiable hatred for Mordecai, Haman devises a plan to destroy him and his entire nation. Using the king's seal, he creates a binding decree in the name of Ahasuerus. Jews are to be exterminated through genocide, according to Haman's plan. He has gallows erected for a mass public hanging and gleefully anticipates their demise at his own hand. Perhaps he is avenging his vanquished Amalekite heritage, perhaps he is taking revenge for his pride injured so by Mordecai—or most likely he is acting out of his rage that may be prompted by a bit of both. Regardless of his motivation, he takes it upon himself to incite the kingdom to wage war against the entire nation of Israel.

Mordecai speaks to Esther privately, warning her that the fate of her people is at stake. He further reminds her of her own danger in the palace once the news of her own heritage is released. She decides she must intervene, for she and Mordecai know that she must have been brought to this position for "such a time as this." She fasts and prays. She earnestly seeks God in the matter and rents her clothing while wallowing in ashes. She humbles herself in contrition before God in anticipation of the great task before her. The existence of her nation lies solely upon her young shoulders. Divine guidance and protection are her only resources.

---

[138] Israel was instructed to eliminate all Amalekites and to "show no mercy," however, at least one survivor remained, from which the bloodline stemmed to Haman. If they had exterminated all the Amalekites as instructed, Haman may never have existed—and the dilemma averted beforehand.

She knows she must approach the king, but to do so incurs a hefty risk—that of possible death. No one is to appear before the king uninvited. She plans a banquet for both the king and Haman. She must request their presence for the event; however, for the delivery of the actual invitation, she must enter the king's court illegally, that is, without a royal summons. The king has already banished a queen who acted impudently, so the situation seems even more risky. Female impertinence at the palace is a distasteful precedent, a dangerously familiar theme that may very well be echoed by Esther's actions, yet she proceeds boldly, making good on her plan.

Noteworthy is this addition to the story, the king suffers from a bout of insomnia. In desperation for sleep, he calls for a reading of the kingdom's records. Mordecai, it is rediscovered, had previously exposed a plot to murder the king, thereby saving the king's life. The king realizes that he was never rewarded properly and decides to remedy this situation. Calling upon his man Haman, he asks for advice as to how he should honor a man that has pleased him. Haman, in his avaricious presumption, goes on to describe what he wishes to be done to himself. He describes his own dreams for himself. He is infuriated when he sees these honors bestowed upon Mordecai. His seething hatred spirals out of control.

Esther summons courage and, at a banquet with the king and Haman, she begs for her life. The surprised king realizes that Haman plans to exterminate all Jews, including his own queen. He makes a new decree that the Jews are allowed to fight back. Haman, in his horror, falls upon Esther, angering the king at his proximity to his queen. He is sent to the gallows himself.

What ensues is a victory for the Jewish people, with Haman and his family all hanged upon the very gallows he ordered to be erected for the Jews. This is a complete victory for the Jewish people at the hand of Esther, and more importantly, a victory by the hand of God who is working silently behind the scenes. This is a Jewish holiday with a recurring theme: "They tried to kill us. We won. Let's eat!" It is a time of festivity and celebration with sobriety and solemnity left far behind!

TRADITIONAL OBSERVANCE

Purim comes in early spring, and is met with much laughter and mirth. Spirits are high and joyous following the dismal winter, and the bright green buds in the world around us further stimulating a frolicking attitude. Puppet shows, costumes, plays, parades and tasty treats are aplenty during this time. Costumes are a big part of the day. Traditionally both children and adults get into the action with every sort of costume imaginable. Although the *Megillah* (basically a scroll containing the entire book *Esther*) is read in the synagogue, *Purim* is only to a lesser degree observed in the confines of holy space; it is more widely celebrated in the streets. Literally is taken the command in scripture, "observe the days [of *Purim*] as days of feasting and joy…"[139]

The "synagogue" part of the day is the traditional reading of the *Megillah*. The *Shechecheyanu* should also be said. It is read with a much different attitude than a typical *Torah* reading, as it is often a boisterous and merry ceremony. The celebrants each bring loud noisemakers (spinning groggers) to use in drowning out the name "Haman" during the reading. Each time Haman's name is read in the story, the raucous congregants yell "boo" while stamping their feet (often with the name "Haman" written on the soles) and spinning the loud clicky groggers. It may sound irreverent, but it is all part of a very deep lesson that is ultimately poignant and stays with the people, old and young alike, generation after generation. The name of Haman (the Amalekite) must be treated thus in accordance to the command, "blot out the remembrance of Amalek."[140] Anti-Semitism is not new, and this story is timeless in its message of hope and triumph for the Jews of today who likewise face enemies and are hated for nothing more than religion and/or nationality.

In Israel, parades and merry-making are almost like a Jewish Mardi Gras, and comparisons have been made; however, the differences are great

---

[139] Esther 9:22
[140] Deuternomy 25:19

between *Purim* and Fat Tuesday. *Purim*, despite all of its fun, is still primarily an educational tool like all Jewish feasts are, passing on the lesson of Esther and Haman to future generations. Mardi Gras is mostly about pre-Lent partying and excess, while *Purim* is in the category of family fun and celebrating the defeat of cultural discrimination and the triumph of God's people in the face of adversity and threatened genocide. *Purim* is a story, a moral and timeless lesson.

Costumes, as stated above, are a main part of *Purim*. Why? It is a "masquerade" theme that is celebrated. It commemorates the "hidden" or "unseen." In the entire book of Esther, the word "God" or any allusion to Him is not mentioned. The series of "coincidences" makes it obvious that God is indeed behind the whole story, working the events to His purpose and to that of the people of Israel's advantage; however, He is never really mentioned. He is disguised and masked, in a way. He is there, and we can clearly see His working, but it is as though He is hidden. Lending also to this theme of disguise is Esther's own secret Jewish identity. Little Hebrew orphan Hadassah, as the Persian Queen Esther, was not openly Jewish until the fate of her people hung in the balance. Both God and Esther have identities that are hidden and unseen, and therefore, likewise are the observers of *Purim*.

Food and drink are obviously a grand part of the celebration. Cookies such as *Hamentaschen* are made—triangle pastries similar to shortbread filled with poppy seeds, jam or a tasty nut-fruit filling. Recently, tradition has added chocolate to this list. Regardless of what fills these delicious little morsels, they are a highlight of *Purim*, especially with the children. They are triangle to commemorate the shape of the villain's head covering in the story—namely Haman's hat. Seeds are a prominent part of the tradition of this day as well. While Queen Esther was in the palace, she was surrounded by unkosher food and unclean meats. She is said to have adopted a diet heavy in seeds and nuts to get her protein while avoiding the many forbidden delicacies of the king's table.

Another part of the tradition is to give out edible gifts to each other. Called *shalach manot* (or sometimes *mishloach manos*), these goody bags are wonderful treats, presents of delicious ready-to-eat food, fun to both give and receive. This fulfills the part of the verse in *Esther* where scripture reads that subsequent generations are to annually, "observe the days as days of … *giving presents of food to one another* and gifts to the poor." The gifts to the poor are usually a minimum of two donations to charity. *Purim* is not a selfish drunken party, but a chance for God's people to remember their history, their salvation, and to pass on blessings to others.

HOW CAN THIS BENEFIT YOU, A CHRISTIAN?

Purim has great significance to the Christian. The *Megillah* read upon this day, the book of *Esther*, closely parallels the life of the Christian. Upon analysis of this book, we can see that God's name is mysteriously missing. Nowhere is God mentioned. He is obviously behind everything—prayers are directed to Him, and simply too many coincidences occur for us to ignore divine intervention.

The absence of metaphysical phenomenon or astonishing manifestations of the supernatural should not cause us to errantly assume that God is absent from the narrative. We may see no burning bushes, no Egyptian plagues, no seas wrought asunder and no walls of Jericho falling; however, God's fingerprints are everywhere. Miracles abound in the book when we consider how the coincidences "just seem to line up" so well, and all in the favor of Esther, Mordecai and the Jewish people. Hadassah, the orphaned little Jewish girl is raised to the queen's throne. Coincidence? Mordecai hears and reports a plot against the king and becomes the hero.

This is cause for retrospection, as are all the biblical and Jewish holidays. Close examination of the Christian life will also render us humbled and in awe of the way God has worked in our lives. We sometimes do not notice the hidden lattice-work in our lives, the way that certain things happen at certain times. Often we might not understand these things and chalk them up to chance when we should be giving credence to the

Master strategist Who works through us and in us to weave our lives into masterpieces that glorify our Heavenly Father and work to mature us in our own walk, our experience in the Word of God.

Often we do not understand why certain things happen in our lives. Disaster strikes. Pain and suffering haunt us. Twists and turns unexpectedly rock our lives. Why do these things happen to us when we are in the palm of God's hands? How can harm reach us? Why do bad things happen to good people?

We cannot see always God's hand in our lives. At times, we cannot feel the comforting and peaceful warmth of His presence, yet He remains. He is not simply with us and holding us, but He is the loom upon which our very lives are woven. Just as a loom holds the threads that make a patterned cloth, so God provides the matrix upon which we are designed. The pattern of our lives, the very identity of who we are and who we become are products of this great invisible loom. The dark threads come into our lives and confound and discourage us. At times, the patterns in our cloth seem to take on foreboding and discouraging forms. Like Mordecai, we are feeling cursed and wronged—dark threads. Like Esther, we are orphaned and alone—more dark threads. We also experience the triumphant times of victory; Haman gets his own gallows. These threads in our lives are bright and shimmering, a glorious contrast to those dark threads on this same piece of cloth. Watching the weaver's work from a distance is the key to seeing the design, the intricate and seemingly random patterns of the light and the dark, the joyous and mournful, the victorious and failing, the euphoric and depressed, all bright and harsh hues are worked together to comprise the magnum opus, the divine design of the Christian life. When observing too closely, in the thick of the flying shuttle and threads, it is all a blur of confusion. If all the threads were alike, all the same bright white, no pattern would emerge. God is making us into beautiful tapestries depicting His own likeness—and thus he needs to use light and dark, bright and subdued, colorful and muted threads to complete the woven portrait of our lives. In Him, all our experiences work together for our good. We cannot see Him at work, but like Esther and Mordecai, we know He is working diligently on our behalf, and by faith, we can trust Him in this.

HOLIDAY NOSHES (SNACKS)

These *Hamentaschen* cookies resemble triangles—the purported shape of Haman's hat. Since the holiday celebrates Esther's reign in the non-kosher palace (therefore using her diet's mainstay of nuts, legumes and seeds as themes), these items are often reflected in the filling.

EASY HAMENTASCHEN (pareve)

Ingredients

- 1/2 cup sugar
- 1/2 cup vegetable oil or vegetable shortening
- 3 eggs
- 2 1/2 teaspoons vanilla
- 5 1/2 cups all-purpose flour
- 3/4 cup orange juice
- 1 tablespoon baking powder
- 1 cup of any flavor jam, fruit preserves

Variation

- 1/2 cup chopped nuts (walnuts, almonds or pecans) may be added to apricot jam for a nutty robust filling.
- Rose or orange blossom essence may be used in lieu of vanilla.
- Poppyseed filling (often available canned) is a popular traditional choice.

Directions

1. Preheat oven to 350 degrees F (175 degrees C). Grease several cookie sheets.
2. In a large bowl, beat the eggs and sugar until fluffy and light.
3. Stir in the oil, vanilla (or essences) and orange juice.
4. Combine the flour and baking powder together thoroughly; stir into the batter to form a stiff dough. If dough is not stiff enough to roll out, add more flour.
5. On a lightly floured surface, roll dough to 1/4 inch thickness.
6. Cut into circles using a cookie cutter or the rim of a coffee mug. Place cookies 2 inches apart onto the prepared cookie sheets.
7. Spoon about 2 teaspoons of filling into the center of each cookie.
8. Fold in three sides to make three corners. The cookie should resemble a triangle with the filling visible in the middle. Overlap each side so that each flap is both over (on one side) and under (on the other side) an adjacent flap. If the sides are only pinched together, they will unfold in the oven. Overlapping them ensures that the cookie holds its shape. If necessary, moisten the dough to ensure that the sides of the dough "stick" together as well.
9. Bake for 12 to 15 minutes in the preheated oven, or until lightly browned. Allow cookies to cool for 1 minute on the cookie sheet before removing to wire racks to cool
10. completely.
11. ENJOY!

Wine is a big part of the *Purim* celebration, however, many adults (not to mention children) do not drink alcoholic beverages. This "wine" is a great substitute!

PURIM "WINE" (pareve)

Combine:

- Lightly stir 1 part club soda (carbonated water) with 1 part grape juice and 2 parts pomegranate juice.
- ENJOY!

Variation:

- Substitute grape juice for mango. Yum!

HOLOCAUST REMEMBRANCE DAY (YOM HASHOAH)

Yom HaShoah means, literally, "Day of Catastrophe," and Holocaust itself refers to a "sacrificial offering consumed by fire." Both terms accurately describe the suffering of the Jewish nation during World War II. Surely it was a Day of Catastrophe when so many of the descendants of Israel were in a very literal sense sacrificed and burned—cremated en masse in horrific furnaces fashioned solely for the destruction of human flesh. This is not a biblical holiday; obviously, it commemorates the Holocaust of World War II and was instituted shortly after Israel proclaimed its own statehood. Despite this, however, we can remind ourselves that anti-Semitism has been prevalent in many areas and times before and after this event in history. The story of *Purim*, featured earlier in this book, is a perfect illustration of a plotted genocide against the Jewish people in ancient times. Anti-Semitism is an unavoidable evil in the world of Jewry even today, however, it does not have to be accepted or tolerated. We must always continue to fight against the ugliness and hatred of both religious and racial prejudice, both of which are involved in anti-Semitism.

Most know the story of the Holocaust initiated by Hitler and his Nazi regime in the late 1930's until the end of the war. At least six million European Jews were cruelly exterminated in the most inhumane methods imaginable.[141] Men, women, children and babies were collectively and individually denied their own rights not only to civil liberties but to *life* in general.

I will not go into details of the history, as it is lengthy, and only a full library can do justice to the tragic topic. The time was a dark one—the darkest in Jewish history. This attempted genocide surpasses even the *"Holy" Inquisition* of the Catholic Church in the fifteenth century and the mass slaughters and crucifixions of Jews by Romans in earlier times.

This time is best commemorated by sobriety and silence in the remembrance of the countless innocents whose lives were so senselessly snatched away by the cruel hands of hatred. Also, we commemorate the desperate heroism of those who participated in the Warsaw Ghetto Uprising. The disbelief, grief and horror can be very overwhelming. I make sure that my children are aware of the event in history, but I am careful to keep overwhelming details and photos away from their fragile comprehension. We use the day to celebrate the lives of those who lived brightly despite the ugliness of the times. We hail the survivors and their stories. We focus on the raw courage and strength of these individuals. We pause to reflect upon the goodness of humanity that shone through in both Jews and Gentiles in an attempt to balance the overwhelming evil.

Unbelievably, many hate groups exist today who are actively working to erase this travesty from history books. The unspeakable murder of over six million Jews is to go undocumented and forgotten if these hate groups are given the credence and power to achieve their agendas. Christians and Jews alike must lobby for truth. We must persevere to keep the memories of these murdered millions alive. Forgetting that they have ever lived is akin to killing them anew.

---

[141] Many innocent Polish Gentiles were also killed.

TRADITIONAL OBSERVANCE

On this day, secular commemorations take place around the United States as well as in Israel and other parts of the world. Synagogues, naturally, offer special services and programs although no official liturgy for the holiday is in place at the writing of this book. Home observances are special, however, as we can tailor them to our own families' needs, especially for the children. The younger generations must be make known of those who have gone before without being traumatized by the magnitude of horror and injustice of the Holocaust. Special emphasis with children must be on *hope* as well as remembrance. This can be achieved by finding and reading stories of the displayed courage and triumphs of both the survivors and of the counter-Nazi work of the Resistance (check your local library and book centers). Yes, a horrible and unthinkable thing has happened, but this is not the end; we can go on with hope and determination to make the world a better place for our being in it.

In Israel, a two-minute siren is sounded at eight o-clock in the morning of the holiday. All buses, commercial trucks, cars, pedestrians, commerce and daily activities stop and freeze during this time of contemplation and remembrance. Then, as suddenly as the siren started, it stops, and life buzzes around immediately after. This symbolizes that the Jewish people, although having suffered, are not conquered. They keep going with strength and purpose, unvanquished by hatred and those who have attempted to extinguish them altogether. The Jewish people keep going.

FAST OF THE NINTH OF AV (TISHA B'AV)

On the Jewish calendar: 9 *Av*

...Should I weep in the fifth month [Av], separating myself like I have done these so many years?[142]

HOLIDAY BACKGROUND

Amidst the joys of the year's celebrations also come heavy days of sorrow. Such is this time of year. *Tisha B'Av* (meaning literally "the ninth of *Av*") is the culmination of a three-week mourning period begun on the 17th of *Tammuz* the month before (commemorating the day that the walls of Jerusalem were first breached by the Romans in 69 C.E.). At *Rosh Chodesh*, or the first day of *Av*, begins the final nine days of the three-week grieving time, bringing with it an intensified state of solemnity. The mourning period climaxes on its final day, *Tisha B'Av*. On this fateful day, Israel has experienced much tragedy including the following:

1. The "bad report" from the twelve spies to Canaan and resulting decree that the nation would therefore not enter the Land[143]

---

[142] Zechariah 7:5
[143] Numbers 13-14 (14:26-35)

2. Destruction and burning of the First Temple (586 B.C.E.)[144]
3. Destruction of the Second Temple including 2.5 million Jewish deaths (70 C.E.)[145]
4. Defeat of the Bar Kochba Revolt (132-135 C.E.) [146]
5. The falling of Betar (132 C.E.)[147]
6. Romans ploughed the Temple Mount to construct the pagan city of Aelia Capitolina in its stead (133 C.E.)[148]
7. The Siege and Razing of Jerusalem (614 C.E.)[149]
8. First Crusade declared by Pope Urban II (1095 C.E.)[150]
9. The Expulsion of Jews from England including the confiscation of all property and burning of sacred texts and writings (1290)[151]
10. The deadline of the Alhambra Decree (1492)[152]

---

[144] II Kings 25:8-9, Jer 52:12-13 Although King Nebuchadnezzar entered the Temple and desecrated it on the 7th of *Av*; it was not actually burned until two days later.
[145] Talmud, *Ta'anit* 29a
[146] Bar Kochba, a charismatic military, considered by many erroneously to be the Messiah, led them to bitter defeat. The fall of Betar (or Bethar) also occurred, killing 100,000. It was the last fortress holding out against the Romans during the Bar Kochba Revolt.
[147] Also called "Bethar," this was the last fortress to hold out against Rome during the Bar Kochba Revolt. The falling of this fortress resulted in at least 100,000 deaths.
[148] This was one year following the fall of Betar
[149] This resulted in countless deaths including at least 90,000 Christians
[150] Over 10,000 Jews were killed in first month alone of the bloody Crusade to reclaim the Holy Land. The Crusades totally obliterated many Jewish communities in Rhineland and France and brought death and destruction to countless other Semitic communities.
[151] King Edward I made an edict that banned all Jews from England as of 1290. This decree was not overturned until 1656.
[152] Also known as the "Edict of Expulsion," this statement by Queen Isabella and King Ferdinand forced all people of Jewish identity out of Spain and its territories. It was not revoked until 1968. Note: If a Jewish calendar is used to convert the date of the Alhambra Decree's deadline for Jewish evacuation (July 31, 1492), the date 27th of *Tammuz* may be the result. If so, the conversion has failed to take into account the Gregorian Reformation which caused a removal of eleven days on the calendar. If the eleven days are added and the date of August 11 is converted instead, we can see that the date is indeed the 9th of *Av*.

11. Germany declared war, beginning events culminating in the Holocaust (1914)
12. Deportation of Warsaw ghetto to Treblinka (1924)[153]
13. Deadly bombing of Buenos Aires Jewish Community Center (1994)[154]
14. Expulsion of Gush Katif/Gaza Strip (2005)
15. II Lebanon War (2006)

TRADITIONAL OBSERVANCE

This mourning period beginning on the 17th of Tammuz until the 9th of Av is a time of forfeiting pleasure while mourning the sadness of the nation's tragedies. Especially on *Tisha B'Av*, the days are observed by a denial of comfort in commemoration of the many losses of Israel this day—the collective sadness of a nation over the ages is made personal. This is a day of fasting. The first pleasures denied on this day are eating and drinking. Like *Yom Kippur*, this includes a prohibition against washing or bathing (only hands up to knuckles). No creams, oils or cosmetics are used. No leather shoes are worn. No music is played or enjoyed. No displays of affection, public or private, are indulged. This also includes a ban on weddings, parties, and trivial gaiety until after the period of mourning is past. Even the *Torah* cabinet (ark) in the synagogue itself is draped in black. Lamentations are read, but no study of the *Torah* is permitted, as the *Torah* is a joyous gift. The time is reserved for mourning and weeping for the sorrows of the past. This is balanced with a cautious look toward the future with earnest prayers to ensure that the days ahead are spared the horror and dread of days past.

Jeremiah conveys the mood of the day with his lament:

---

[153] This resulted in well over 56,000 deaths.
[154] 86 Jewish people died with 300 more injured.

Restore us to you, O LORD,
that we may be restored;
Renew our days as of old,
Unless You have utterly rejected us
And are exceedingly angry with us.[155]

HOW CAN THIS BENEFIT YOU, A CHRISTIAN?

Yeshua is believed by some to have fasted in the wilderness during this time, with his temptations falling upon or around *Tisha B'Av*. Why is this? The Jewish calendar has assigned *Torah* readings throughout the year. Each week has its own assigned text—that never changes. When we look at the answers that Yeshua gave to the tempter in the wilderness, they all came from *Deuteronomy* chapters six through eight. Interestingly enough, these passages appear in close proximity in the *Torah* readings. Therefore, if these were also the *Torah* readings of the time of year that Yeshua quoted them, the theory holds that perhaps they occurred during the time of *Tisha B'Av*. This would be quite logical, as *Tisha B'Av* is a time of fasting for the woes of Israel past and present. Yeshua fasted on account of the woes and judgments of Israel past and future—to include the believers "grafted into" the nation. Whether or not this theory is true, we can always benefit from stopping and pondering the story of Yeshua and the temptations in the wilderness as well as the texts he used to refute the Tempter. How can we recognize such temptation in our own lives? How do we find hope in the midst of tragedy? Where is our stronghold?

---

[155] Lamentations 5:21-22, NASB

CONCLUSION

It is truly my hope and desire that as a Christian, you will be able to appreciate and even implement some of these treasures, these holiday lessons, in your life. God's appointed days are all so full of meaning and lessons that can benefit and even transform any Christian's walk into an even sweeter experience.

Whether you find yourself smiling at the sweet aroma of *challah* bread and later of cloves on Sabbath, singing during a *seder*, staying up in the night reading the *Torah* while eating dairy *noshes*, blowing a *shofar* by the river while enjoying the liberation of *Tashlich*, singing with family and friends over a meal in a colorfully decorated *sukkah*, recalling miracles by candlelight and *dreidel* games, enjoying the giddy silliness of hollering "boo" with abandon while wildly swinging loud groggers during the reading of the *Purim Megillah*, or dancing joyously with the word of God, my prayer is that you will find the joys that I have. It is my desire that you will find an even more intimate walk with your Creator—an even deeper intimacy with your Jewish Messiah who is the focus and fulfillment of these sacred times.

WEEKLY PARSHA READINGS

The *Torah* is divided up into weekly readings that span the year.

Parshah	Torah
Bereishit	Genesis 1:1-6:8
Noach	Genesis 6:9-11:32
Lekh Lekha	Genesis 12:1-17:27
Vayeira	Genesis 18:1-22:24
Chayei Sarah	Genesis 23:1-25:18
Toldot	Genesis 25:19-28:9
Vayeitzei	Genesis 28:10-32:3
Vayishlach	Genesis 32:4-36:43
Vayyeshev	Genesis 37:1-40:23
Miqeitz	Genesis 41:1-44:17
Vayigash	Genesis 44:18-47:27
Vayechi	Genesis 47:28-50:26
Shemot	Exodus 1:1-6:1
Va'eira	Exodus 6:2-9:35

Bo	Exodus 10:1-13:16
Beshalach	Exodus 13:17-17:16
Yitro	Exodus 18:1-20:23
Mishpatim	Exodus 21:1-24:18
Terumah	Exodus 25:1-27:19
Tetzaveh	Exodus 27:20-30:10
Ki Tisa	Exodus 30:11-34:35
Vayaqhel	Exodus 35:1-38:20
Pequdei	Exodus 38:21-40:38
Vayiqra	Leviticus 1:1-5:26
Tzav	Leviticus 6:1-8:36
Shemini	Leviticus 9:1-11:47
Tazria	Leviticus 12:1-13:59
Metzora	Leviticus 14:1-15:33
Acharei Mot	Leviticus 16:1-18:30
Qedoshim	Leviticus 19:1-20:27
Emor	Leviticus 21:1-24:23
Behar	Leviticus 25:1-26:2
Bechuqotai	Leviticus 26:3-27:34
Bamidbar	Numbers 1:1-4:20
Nasso	Numbers 4:21-7:89
Beha'alotkha	Numbers 8:1-12:16
Shelach	Numbers 13:1-15:41
Qorach	Numbers 16:1-18:32

*Chuqa*t	Numbers 19:1-22:1
*Bala*q	Numbers 22:2-25:9
*Pincha*s	Numbers 25:10-30:1
*Matto*t	Numbers 30:2-32:42
*Mase*i	Numbers 33:1-36:13
*Devari*m	Deuteronomy 1:1-3:22
*Va'etchana*n	Deuteronomy 3:23-7:11
*Eiqe*v	Deuteronomy 7:12-11:25
*Re'e*h	Deuteronomy 11:26-16:17
*Shofti*m	Deuteronomy 16:18-21:9
*Ki Teitze*i	Deuteronomy 21:10-25:19
*Ki Tav*o	Deuteronomy 26:1-29:8
*Nitzavi*m	Deuteronomy 29:9-30:20
*Vayeilek*h	Deuteronomy 31:1-31:30
*Ha'azin*u	Deuteronomy 32:1-32:52
*Vezot Haberakh*ah	Deuteronomy 33:1-34:12

BIBLIOGRAPHY
& Recommended Further Reading:

Benyosef, S. (1999). *Living the Kabbalah.* New York: The Continuum Publishing Company.

Burstein, Abraham. (1940). *A Jewish Child's Garden of Verses.* New York: Bloch Publishing Company.

Booker, R. (2009). *Celebrating Jesus in the Biblical Feasts.* Shippensburg, PA: Destiny Image Publishers.

Cordoza, A. (1982). *Jewish Family Celebrations: The Sabbath, Festivals & Ceremonies.* New York: St. Martin's Press.

Drucker, M. &. (1994). *The Family Treasure of Jewish Holidays.* New York: Little Brown & Co.

Felton, R. (Accessed 24 Apr 2010). Children. *Potter's Clay Ministries .* www.haydid.org/pot3.htm.

Fischer, J. (2004, accessed 04 Aug 2010). The Meaning and Importance of the Jewish Holidays. *Menorah*

Ministries . www.menorahministries.com/Scriptorium/MeaningOfHolidays.htm.

Hillel, Y. (Accessed 25 Apr 2010). Shabbat the Central Light. *Torah.Org* . www.torah.org/features/holydays/centrallight.html#coments.

Howard, Kevin & Marvin Rosenthal. (1997). *The Feasts of the Lord: God's Prophetic Calendar from Calvary to the Kingdom.* Zion's Hope, Inc.

Katz, L. (accessed 12 May 2010). All About Judaism's Sabbath Candles. *About.Com: Judaism.* judaism.about.com/od/sabbath 1/p/all_ nerot.htm.

McQuaid, E. (1990). *The Outpouring: Jesus in the Feasts of Israel.* Bellmawr: NJ: The Friends of Israel Gospel Ministry.

Sampson, R. &. (1999). *A Family Guide to the Biblical Holidays.* Stafford, VA: Heart of Wisdom Publishing, Inc.

Schauss, H. (1975). *The Jewish Festivals.* New York: Schocken Books.

Scott, B. (1997). *The Feasts of Israel.* Bellmawr, NJ: The Friends of the Gospel Ministry.

Simcha, B. (Accessed 12 May 2010). Is There a Specific Way to Hold the Kiddush Cup? *Askmoses.com* . www.askmoses.com/en/article/204,2082884/Is-there-a-specific-way-to-hold-the-Kiddush-cup.html.

Steinburg, P. (2007). *Chelebrating the Jewish Year.* Philadelphia: The Jewish Publication Society.

Strassfeld, M. (1985). *The Jewish Holidays: A Guide & Commentary.* New York: Harper & Row.

Waskow, A. (1982). *Seasons of our Joy.* New York: Summit Books.

BIBLES USED [156]

NIV: NEW INTERNATIONAL VERSION®. Copyright © 1973, 1978, 1984. Biblica.

NASB: New American Standard Bible. Copyright © 1960, 1962, 1963, 1968, 1971, 1972, 1973, 1975, 1977, 1995 by The Lockman Foundation, La Habra, Calif.

---

[156] Since this is a Christian handbook, I have used Christian Bibles as opposed to Jewish.

www.ingramcontent.com/pod-product-compliance
Lightning Source LLC
Chambersburg PA
CBHW051923160426
43198CB00012B/2019